Letters and Numbers

(This page is for practising writing the letters and numbers)

Capital letters

A B C D E F G H I
J K L M N O P Q R
S T U V W X Y Z

Lower case letters

a b c d e f g h i
j k l m n o p q r
s t u v w x y z

Numbers

0 1 2 3 4 5 6 7
8 9 10 11 12...

English

for living in Britain

Books 1 and 2 combined edition

English

for living in Britain

Books 1 and 2 combined edition

Ian Sydenham

Note to teachers

Welcome to this edition, which uses much of the material previously published in *English for Living in Britain* and *More English for Living in Britain*. Whereas the previous editions were collections of handouts – sometimes not in a logical order – this volume aims to be useful as a coursebook. Many learners will be able to skip through the earlier chapters quickly, but by the end of the volume the complete range of verb tenses will have been presented and learners will have faced up to many of the challenges of learning English.

For most of the units here, especially the example dialogues, I would encourage teachers to spend enough time on practice and repetition. I can be guilty of rushing to ask students to produce language in an unstructured context, only to find that the material has not been sufficiently mastered.

One of the aims has been to present language in context as much as possible. Many courses do this, including much of the BBC Learning English materials, which I often recommend to my classes for follow-up work. The temptation, especially in the presentation of grammar, is to present the learner with a string of unrelated sentences for practice. Grammar without context can become a puzzle without clues. Furthermore, it can neglect any sense of the importance of frequency; for example, ten sentences all practising the third conditional may be of some use to the learner in mastering 'would have, 'should have' etc., but could leave the learner with the impression that this is a frequent, vital structure that he or she should be using every day. This is particularly true of verb tenses, where an over-use of present continuous or past continuous tenses is the result of labouring these in classes, when in practice they are far less frequent than simple present or simple past verbs.

Teachers (or helpers) will need to present some of the material, thereby providing some listening practice. For conversations (as in Unit 24 "Making an appointment", for example), it should be easy enough to make up the missing details for your learners to listen out for. Where there is a topic to present (as in Unit 87 "British history"), I have usually included a script for presentation at the end of the unit, with the intention that learners do not look at this until after they have listened to the presentation and done the accompanying listening exercise.

I hope you enjoy using this volume, and perhaps more importantly, I hope your learners benefit from using it!

Contents

1. Greetings!

Hello! Hi!

Good morning! (before 12.00)

Good afternoon! (from 12.00 to 18.00)

Good evening! (after 18.00)

Pleased to meet you!

What is your name?

My name is _____

Where are you from?

I come from _____

Where do you live?

I live in _____

Numbers:

Say the numbers

1 2 3 4 5 6

1 one   2 two   3 three   4 four   5 five   6 six

2. Objects

Say the words with your teacher

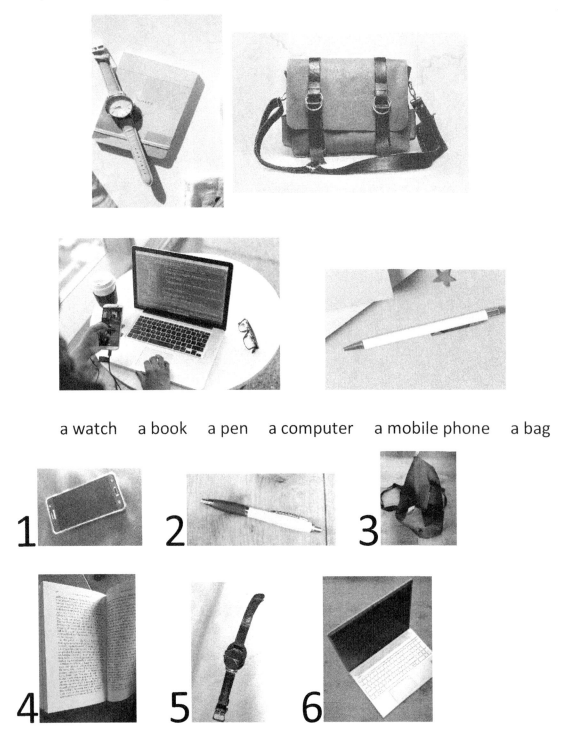

a watch   a book   a pen   a computer   a mobile phone   a bag

Your teacher says the object, you say the number. Then your teacher will say the number, and you say the object.

Your teacher will show you an object – if the object matches the word, repeat it! If it doesn't match, don't say it!

Then you say the word when your teacher shows you the object!

Short conversations:

Practise saying these sentences with your teacher:

Do you have a computer?

No, I don't have a computer, but I have a mobile phone.

Do you need a bag?

No, it's OK – I have a bag.

Sorry, I don't have a pen. Do you have a pen, please?

Here you are!

Thank you!

You're welcome!

3. Numbers, food and drink, likes and dislikes

More Numbers:

7   8   9   10   11   12...

seven   eight   nine   ten   eleven   twelve

0 (zero, oh)

Say these telephone numbers:

01289 734508

07177 265360

08997 321456

Write down the numbers that your teacher or your partner gives you

Food and Drink

What number is ...?

I like

I don't like

I like... I don't like...	pizza chicken apples bananas cake ice cream bread cheese tea coffee oranges/orange juice eggs

Draw some other food and drink that you like and ask your teacher for the words in English.

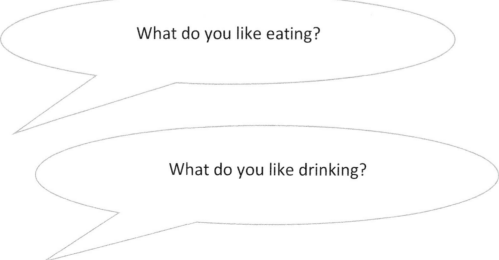

What do you like eating?

What do you like drinking?

"like" + verb

I like eat**ing** pizza.

I like play**ing** football.

I like watch**ing** sport on TV.

Normally we use verb +ing after "like" or "don't like"

I like play**ing** tennis but I don't like watch**ing** it on TV.

Say three things you like eating and one thing you don't like!

Example: "I like fish, and I like potatoes, and I like cheese. I don't like cabbage."

Then say three things you like doing and one thing you don't like doing.

Example: "I like cycling, and I like playing tennis. I like watching films, but I don't like cleaning my room."

4. Brothers and sisters

 I have one brother and one sister.

 I have a sister. I don't have a brother.

 I have three brothers. I don't have a sister.

 I have three brothers and two sisters.

(We can say "half-brother" or "half-sister" if you share one parent.)

 I am an only child – I don't have any brothers or sisters.

Talk about brothers and sisters with your class or a partner.

5. Introducing yourself

- My name is _____ _____.   NAME

- I live in _____   TOWN

- I come from _____   ORIGIN

- I have a brother/two brothers/a sister...   FAMILY

- I like playing sport/watching TV/eating pizza   LIKE?

Use the words on the right to memorise the sentences.

Use the sentences to answer these questions:

What's your name?

What food do you like?

Where do you come from?

Where do you live now?

Do you have any brothers or sisters?

What activities do you like?

Now ask another person the questions.

6. What time is it? More numbers

It's four o'clock

It's nine o'clock

Say the numbers with your teacher:

15	20	30	40	45	50	60
fifteen	twenty	thirty	forty	forty-five	fifty	sixty

What time is it?

5.45

10.15

Say these times: "twelve thirty" ...

12.30   4.00   2.30   20.20   6.15

7. Conversation at the checkout

(You will need to practise numbers and prices)

Shopkeeper: Do you need a bag?

Customer: Yes please. How much are they?

Shopkeeper: They are 10p each

Customer: Just one please.

Shopkeeper: So that's (4 pound 80) please

Customer: Do you have change of (twenty pounds)?

SK: Yes, that's fine... So that's (£15.20) change.

Customer: Thank you. Goodbye.

Shopkeeper: Have a nice day!

Customer: Thank you! You too!

Change roles, change the prices and practise several times!

8. Responses

Practise this conversation:

> Hello. I'm (Alex).
> Pleased to meet you!

> Pleased to meet you too! My name is (Maria).

> How are you?

> Fine, thank you. And you?

> Not bad, thanks

Which response from the box fits ?

Have a nice day!

Thank you!

How are you?

What's your favourite food?

What's your favourite sport?

Do you need a bag?

Pleased to meet you!

Fine, thank you	You're welcome!
Chicken and chips	Football
No, it's OK.	Thank you, you too!
Pleased to meet you too!	

9. Talking about a place

Match the pictures!

 a.

 b.

 c.

 d.

 e.

 f.

a. _____   a shop

b. _____   a church/ a cathedral

c. _____   a café/ a restaurant

d. _____   a castle

e. _____   a park/ a garden

f. _____   a museum/ an art gallery

Practise saying the letters 'a', 'b', 'c', 'd', 'e', 'f'. When your teacher says a place, you say the letter. Then work in pairs, one of you says the place, the other says the letter.

*Pronouncing longer words: The **bold** type marks the strong part of the word:*

mus**e**um

cath**e**dral

r**e**staurant

g**a**llery

Colchester

(There are a lot of new words here – try to guess their meaning and do questions 1-5 before you use a dictionary to check the meaning of some words.)

Colchester is a city in the south-east of England. It has a lot of historical remains – some of them are two thousand years old. There is a castle. The castle is in a large park near the centre of the city. There is a shopping centre, some beautiful churches, a few museums and a lot of cafés and restaurants. The population is about a hundred and fifty thousand (150 000). Some people live in Colchester and work in London. The city is about 60 miles from London, and there is a good train service. The main station is in the north of the city. There is an airport about 30 miles from Colchester.

Complete these sentences – choose (a), (b) or (c):

1. Colchester is (a) a village (b) a town (c) a city.

2. There is (a) a castle (b) a cathedral (c) an airport.

3. There are a lot of (a) museums (b) historical remains (c) stations.

4. There is an airport (a) in the city centre (b) near the city centre (c) 30 miles from the city.

5. Some people go to London most days to (a) work (b) see the famous sights (c) play football.

Nouns normally have 'a' before singular but nothing* before plurals:

There is a mosque/ There are mosques.

There is a school/ There are schools.

There is a shop/ There are shops.

*Before a plural, there can be a number e.g. There are 3 pubs. *You may also find phrases like* "a few", "a couple of" *or* "some"

Before a vowel, we use 'an' to make it easier to say:

There is an airport. There is an art gallery.

25

To make the sentence negative, we normally use 'no' + plural:

There are no pubs.

There are no airports.

There are no churches.

(*Compare the sentence:* "I have a sister but no brothers")

It is also possible to use "There is not/There isn't ..." or "It does not have..."

Some sentences about a village, a town or a city :

The town (or city) is called _____	
There is a castle/ a museum/ a station/a primary school	There is...
There are parliament buildings/shops/cafés/schools	There are...
There are no churches/mosques/temples/schools/shops	There are no...
It has a station/ an airport	It has...
It doesn't have a station/an airport	It doesn't have...

Try to complete this text about the village of Dunchurch. When you see __(1)__, what word is missing? Be careful – three answers have no word missing!

> *Dunchurch is __(1)__ large village in the middle of England. There are __(2)__ shops, three__(3)__pubs, and __(4)__ old church, but there are __(5)__ mosques. There is __(6) primary school, but there are __(7)__ secondary schools. The children over the age of 11 go to __(8)__ secondary schools in Rugby.*

Check your answers:

Which numbers have no word in the space? _____ , _____, and _____

Did you write "an" for any of the answers?

Try to describe Dunchurch without looking at the book, then describe a town or city you know. Keep your sentences simple!

10. Questions

A game: *find a person who answers "Yes" for these questions:*

1. Do you like watching rugby?   _____

2. Do you play tennis?   _____

3. Do you play a musical instrument?   _____

4. Do you like eating fish?   _____

5. Do you have two children?   _____

6. Are you vegetarian?   _____

7. Does your country have a president?   _____

8. Do you normally go to bed before ten o'clock? _____

9. Are you from another continent (not Europe)? _____

10. Do you live near here (less than a mile)? _____

Report your answers like this:

(James) is a vegetarian.

(Sarah) like**s** watching rugby.

(Ahmed) go**es** to bed before ten o'clock.

(Chuck)'s country ha**s** a president.

Can you complete the questions with the missing word from the box?

1. What _____ your name?

2. Where _____ you come from?

3. Where _____ you live?

4. What _____ you do?

5. _____ you interested in (politics)?

6. _____ you have any brothers or sisters?

7. _____ (your brother) live in England?

8. How old _____ you?*

9. What _____ you do in your free time?

*It is not always polite to ask someone this question!

do   does   is   are

*Like negatives, we use **do/does** to make questions with most verbs:*

What sports **do** you play?

What **do** you like eating?

Where **does** your brother live?

*But with **am/are/is** there is no **do/does***

Are you OK?

What is your favourite TV programme?

Practise asking the questions to other students.

11. Talking about another person

Remember that the verb usually ends in -s when we talk about another person or thing.

1. This   is   my friend _____. (*name*)

2. He/she   comes   from _____.

3. He/she   lives   in (Rugby).

4. He/she   is   a (student).

5. He/she   is (not)   married/He is a widower/She is a widow.

6. He/she   has   2 brothers/a sister and a brother/...

7. They   are called   _____, _____, _____, and _____

8. He/she   is   14 (years old)*

9. He/she   likes   playing football/watching TV/walking.

10. He/she   is (not)   interested in (politics)

* Only use sentence 8 for a young person

Remember to use 'does not' for a negative sentence:

He/she does not work at the moment.

He/she does not have any brothers or sisters.

Except for 'is

He/she is not married.

Practise the sentences again: put a finger over the verbs and try to remember them!

Homework: Write 10 sentences about yourself, then ten sentences about two other people – 30 sentences altogether!

12. Revision: Likes and dislikes

Sometimes we just say the thing e.g. food

> I like chicken. I don't like beef.

> My friend likes carrots. She doesn't like cabbage.

With a verb, we use -ing:

> I like play**ing** football. I don't like listen**ing** to music.

> My brother likes play**ing** computer games, but he doesn't like read**ing**.

Make sentences using these verbs to help you.

watch	play	cycle	read	clean
walk	shop	make	sleep	swim

When we write, a verb ending -e loses the -e when we add -ing:

> make – making, cycle – cycling, have – having, take – taking etc.

I like cycling. My son also likes cycling.

30

13. Revision: Talking about another person

This	___	my friend _____. (name)
1. He/she	____	from _____.
2. He/she	____	in (Rugby).
3. He/she	___	a student.
4. He/she	___ (not)	married.
5. He/she	____	2 brothers/a sister and a brother/
6. They	____	called _____, _____, _____, and _____
7. He/she	___	14 (years old)*
8. He/she	____	playing football/watching TV/walking.
9. He/she	___ (not)	interested in (politics).

"his" = belongs to a male

"her"= belongs to a female

[Talking about a male] "He has one brother and two sisters. His brother is called Peter, and his sisters are called Jane and Mary. His brother, Peter, and his sister, Jane, are twins!"

[Talking about a female] "She likes music. Her favourite singer is …"

14. Can you spell that, please? (Alphabet)

Answer these questions:

What is your first name?

And your surname?

What's your postcode?

When you give information about yourself (for example, when you register with a doctor or a dentist), you may have to spell your name. The other person may say **"Can you spell that, please?"**

Look at the letters of the alphabet at the beginning of the book, and say them with your teacher.

The table below groups the letters by sound:

Alphabet

Ee	Bb	Cc	Dd	Gg	Pp	Tt	Vv		as in thr**ee**
Ff	Ll	Mm	Nn	Ss	Xx	Zz			as in s**e**ven
Ii	Yy								as in f**i**ve
Oo									as in J**o**e
Aa	Hh	Jj	Kk						as in c**a**ke
Uu	Qq	Ww							as in y**ou**
Rr									as in **are**

Now answer the questions again, and spell the names:

What is your first name?

Can you spell that, please?

And your surname?

Can you spell that, please?

What's your postcode?

*You will also need to understand when other people spell names and addresses. Listen to your teacher or a helper – he or she will spell some names for you. Write what you hear on paper or a whiteboard. If necessary say: **"Can you repeat that, please?"***

Can you spell that, please?

Yes, it's _ _ _ _ _ _   _ _ _ _ _ _ _ _

Can you repeat that, please?

Certainly – _ _ _ _ _ _ _   _ _ _ _ _

15. At the market

(Market trader): Good afternoon. What would you like?

> *(Customer): Good afternoon. I would like three bananas please.*

Three bananas... here you are. Anything else?

> *Do you have any mangoes?*

I'm sorry, no, we don't have any.

> *OK. Just the bananas please*

That's 80 pence then

> *Eighty or eighteen?*

Eighty!

> *Here you are!*

Thank you. Have a nice day!

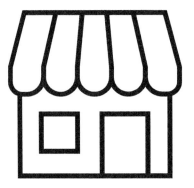

Read the conversation several times – change the fruit and vegetables and the prices, and at the end check that you have understood the other person.

16. More on negative verbs

With most verbs, we make a negative with "do not"

> I like pizza, but I do not like mushrooms.

Often, "do not" is shortened to "don't"

> I don't like this film. I don't like the actors. I don't like the violence...

> I have two brothers, but they don't live in England.

If you speak or write about another person, use "does not" or "doesn't"

> My brother _____ doesn't like football.

> My friend _____ doesn't live in Rugby – he lives in Birmingham.

Exceptions: when we do not use "do/does":

1. *With the verb "to be" (am/is/are)*

   I am not English.

   My friend is not happy.

   John and Mary are not here today.

2. *With verbs like can, must, will, should, may... (called "modal verbs")*

   I cannot (usually shortened **"can't")** understand this document.

   I will not be at the class on Thursday.

   We may not leave the hotel at the moment.

3. *With complex verb tenses (we will study these later!!)*

   I have not lived in England for very long.

   You are not listening!

watch	play	cycle	read	clean
walk	shop	make	sleep	swim

Use the verbs in the box to make more sentences about yourself, positive or negative! Here is an example:

I play football but I don't cycle. I walk to the supermarket. In the evenings I watch films on the computer. I don't read very much. I don't sleep very well here – I must make an effort to exercise more.

Reminder: we also use '**do/does**' to make questions

What **does** this man **like** doing? – He likes painting.

17. Countries (1)

Listen to your teacher saying the countries:

Europe

The United Kingdom

France

Germany

Italy

Portugal

Spain

Some words only have one syllable: France, Spain

When a word has more than one syllable, we normally stress one of the syllables:

G**er**many

The Un**i**ted K**i**ngdom

P**or**tugal

Try saying these countries and continents – the stress is marked for you:

The N**et**herlands

Est**oni**a*

Slov**en**ia*

Africa

Asia

The Un**i**ted St**at**es

C**an**ada

A lot of countries end -ia*, and the stress falls on the syllable before -ia

Albania, Australia, Slovakia, Serbia, Lithuania, Latvia, Russia, Croatia, Mauritania, India, Ethiopia, (*but* Tanzan**ia** *is an exception*).

18. Family

Check these words with your teacher or a dictionary:

son	daughter
brother	sister
father	mother
wife	husband
partner	
grandson	granddaughter
grandfather	grandmother

Use "my" to talk about your family.

Example: My mother is called Selina. My son is called Yuri…

This is Jack. He is 51 years old, he is married and he has two children. His wife, Sarah, works in a bank. His son's name is Bradley, and his daughter's name is Britney. Bradley lives with his partner, Kylie, and they have a daughter, Emma (Jack and Sarah's granddaughter). Britney does not have any children.

Jack's father died a few years ago, but his mother is still alive, so she is now a great-grandmother! Jack has a brother, David, and a sister, Helen.

Fill in words from the box to complete the sentences:

son	daughter
brother	sister
father	mother
wife	husband
partner	
grandson	granddaughter

1. Bradley is Jack's _____.

2. Sarah is Jack's _____.

3. Emma is Jack's _____.

4. David is Jack's _____.

5. Helen is Jack's _____.

6. Kylie is Bradley's _____ and Emma's _____.

Imagine you are Jack! Can you see what words are missing from this presentation?

Hello! My name is Jack. I ____ 51, I _____ married and I _____ two children. My son, Bradley, lives with his partner and they have a daughter, so now I ____ a grandfather. I ____ not have a grandson. My daughter, Britney, _____ not have any children I _____ an older brother, David, and a sister, Helen. She ____ younger than me. My wife ____ called Sarah.

What can you say about your family?

Do you know what a family tree is? Draw your family tree here (or on a piece of paper), then talk about it to another person.

Example: This is me. I have a grandmother but I don't have a grandfather. My parents are called _____ and _____. I have a brother and two sisters. They are called _____, ____, and _____. My brother_____ is married and has one son. My sister _____ is not married but she lives with her partner. They do not have any children. My other sister_____ is not married – she is only 16 years old.

19. Café Conversation

What can I get you?

Hello. Can I have a cup of coffee, please?

Would you like an americano, a cappuccino, or an espresso?

Just a simple white coffee please

Any sugar?

Yes please, one.

Anything else?

No thank you.

That's two pounds thirty

Here you are.

Thank you, Enjoy your drink!

a knife and a fork   a spoon

a teaspoon a cup and saucer   a mug

a plate    a dish/a bowl

Add to the café conversation: Can I have a spoon/plate/bowl..., please?

20. Time words

There are 365 days in a year.

There are 7 days in a week.

There are 52 weeks in a year.

There are 24 hours in a day.

There are 60 minutes in an hour.

There are 60 seconds in a minute.

There are 12 months in the year, but they are not all the same.

January, March, May, July, August, October and December have 31 days.

April, June, September and November have 30 days.

February normally has 28 days, but every four years there is an extra day – the 29th of February. We call these years "leap years". 2024 is a leap year.

Complete the sentences:

60 seconds make a _____(1)_____.

There are 24 hours in a __(2)___.

February normally has __(3)__ days.

There are 365 days in a __(4)___.

Four months have __(5)__ days.

The parts of the day

Morning lasts until 12 noon

Between 12 noon and about 6.00 pm is called the **afternoon**.

The **evening** lasts from 6.00 pm until bedtime.

Night is the time when we sleep.

*What do you do **in** the morning? What do you do **at** night? What do you do **in** the evening?*

21. Silent letters: Is "right" the same as "write"?

It can be difficult to pronounce words because some letters are silent:

write – *we do not pronounce the 'w', so it sounds the same as "right".*

know – *we do not pronounce the 'k'*

These two examples help you to pronounce these words – now try!

wrist, knee, knife, wrap, wrong, knit, knock,...

'igh' has a silent 'g' – we pronounce it like the letter 'i' in the alphabet. Try these words:

light, sigh, night, bright, thigh

The letter 'h' is sometimes silent, but not usually! These words have a silent 'h':

hour, honest, honour,

but we pronounce the 'h' most of the time:

home, head, heart,

If it is silent, you will hear and see 'an' before it:

an hour, half an hour...

but most words beginning with 'h' have 'a':

a home, a hospital ...

You have also seen the word "castle", which has a silent 't'

Try reading this text out loud: there are at least four silent letters!

Warwick Castle is fantastic. You can learn a lot about English history. You see people dressed as knights, fighting for the honour of their king. Others dress as princes and princesses. You need about four hours to visit it – there is a lot to see!

You will need to copy what you hear – it isn't easy to make rules about silent letters!

22. Review: Basic sentences

The Subject - the person or the thing doing the verb

The Verb – the action, the doing word

The rest of the sentence sometimes includes an Object – the person or thing receiving the verb

Subject	Verb	Object?	Rest of sentence
I	am		pleased to meet you!
I	need	help	with my English.
I	wear	a tracksuit	
My daughter	wears	a skirt	to school.

Negatives:

am/is/are not

Other verbs: do/does not + 'verb'

Subject	Negative verb	Object?	Rest of sentence
My son	is not		here today.
He	does not go		to school yet.
We	do not have	enough clothes	
My daughter	does not have	sport shoes	

Modal verbs *can/will/must/may*: **no 'do/does'**

I will not be here next lesson

I can't (=can not) come to the lesson next week

Fill in the missing words in this text:

My friend _____ from Africa. He does ____ speak English, but he will ____ to lessons. We ____ not have enough clothes. I need some shoes and my friend _____ not have any gloves. I _____ pleased to be here, but it ____ cold at night.

Missing words: is   am   do   does   come   comes   not

23. Days and months

Say the days after your teacher:

Monday

Tuesday

Wednesday

Thursday

Friday

Saturday

Sunday

The months of the year:

January

February

March

April

May

June

July

August

September

October

November

December

Dates

The first of...   , The second of ...,   The third of ..., The fourth of ..., The fifth of..

*Normally we add -**th** to the number, but as well as 'first/second/third' you need*
to think about 'twenty-first, twenty-second, twenty-third, thirty-first'
You will see "21st, 22nd, 23rd then 24th, 25th ..."

If '1' (or '01') is January, and '12' is December, practise saying these dates

Example: 23/05 = the twenty-third of May

    25/12

    06/06

    03/11

    13/08

    2/07

    31/05

    22/10

    11/09

When is your birthday?

> My birthday is the twenty-first of April

Ask five other people "When is your birthday?"

If we ask "When is your birthday?", we don't expect to be told the year of your birth! If you are giving information in a formal situation (you apply for a driving licence, a passport, a bank account, an insurance policy...), you will hear the question "What is your date of birth?" In this situation, it is quite usual just to give numbers, for example:

- What's your date of birth, please?
- It's 07/10/92

Or you could say "The seventh of October nineteen ninety two"

24. Making an appointment

(You will need to practise the alphabet)

Read the conversation about making an appointment

with a hairdresser:

(The client):

Hello.

(The receptionist)

Good morning, what can I do for you?

Can I make an appointment, please?

Yes, what day?

Can I come tomorrow?

Sorry, tomorrow is fully booked.

What about (____day), the (date) ?
Example: seventh of February

Yes, (____day) you can come at (10.30)

Yes, (10.30) is fine.

Can I have your name please?

It's _____ _____ (name)

Can you spell that, please?

That's _ _ _ _ _ _ _ _ _ _ _ _
(spell the name)

Thank you. That's booked for you on ____day the ____ of (month) at (time).

Thank you very much. See you on (____day) at _____ (time).

Goodbye!

Goodbye!

Read the conversation again but change the details!

25. Tell me about yourself!

My name is _____ _____.	NAME
I come from _____.	COUNTRY
It is a country in _____. (e.g. Europe, Africa...)	CONTINENT
Now I live in _____.	TOWN
I am (not) married.	MARRIED?
I have _____ and _____.	FAMILY?
(a son, two sons, a brother, a sister, two sisters etc.)	
I do not have any_____	DON'T HAVE
(children, grandchildren, brothers, sisters)	
I work in a(n) _____ OR I do not work.	WORK
I am retired/unemployed/a student/a housewife*/ a househusband.	ALTERNATIVES
I like _____ing (_____).	ACTIVITY ♡
...but I don't like _____ing. (_____)	ACTIVITY 🗇
My favourite food is _____	FOOD ♡
I also like _____ and _____.	FOOD 🗇
...but I don't like _____.	

*'housewife' is a bit old-fashioned: you can also say "I am a stay-at-home mum"

Practise saying the sentences. Try to use the word on the right to help memorise them.

*Which sentence fits which question? Use one of your sentences above to answer these questions. When the question has *, you need to start your answer with "Yes" or "No".*

- What do you like eating?
- Do you work?*
- What do you do?
- Where do you come from?
- Are you married?*
- Do you have any brothers or sisters?*
- What activities do you like?
- Where do you live?

- What's your name?

26. The seasons and weather

Spring is in the months of March, April and May

Summer is in June, July and August

Autumn is in September, October and November

Winter is in December, January and February

Weather expressions

It is + adjective

It is	hot/cold/sunny/cloudy/foggy/rainy/snowy/mild...

'rain' and 'snow' can also be verbs

It	rains/snows
It	is raining/is snowing (at the moment)

In my country it snows in December.

It is raining today.

What's the weather like?

Today it is ...

The temperature is about _____ degrees (Centigrade).

What is the weather like in Britain in May?

It is quite sunny and not too cold. Sometimes it rains.

What is the weather like in Britain in winter?

What is the weather like in _____ (your home country) in _____
(month/season)?

27. Talking about TV and films

What kind of television programme do you like watching?

My favourite programme is _____.

(I don't have a favourite programme, but I like watching _____.)

It	is	a	comedy sports news documentary nature quiz home design reality	programme.
It	is	a		gameshow. series. drama. competition.
The main person The main people	is are	_____		
It	is	(very)	funny/exciting/beautiful/tense/ informative/interesting	

Can you describe the programme simply? Here are some examples...

It is a competition. The participants try to cook something very well and some judges decide who is the best.

It is a comedy programme. The main person is the comedian _____ _____, and he gets himself into difficult situations. It's always very funny.

It is a series. Every time the programme finishes, we wonder what will happen next.

It's a nature programme. The main person is called Sir David Attenborough. The photography is beautiful, and it is usually very interesting.

Answer these questions about the programme:

> When is it on?
>
> What channel is it on?
>
> Do you watch it live or on catch-up?
>
> Do you normally watch it with someone else?
>
> Do you recommend the programme?

... and some more questions about your enjoyment of television:

> Do you watch a lot of television?
>
> Do you prefer the TV or watching things on the computer?
>
> What kind of programme do you *not* like?

Can you use the same language to describe films? What is your favourite film? Who is your favourite actor?

It	is	a	science-fiction	film. romance. thriller. comedy.
The main character	is...			
The main characters	are...			
It	is		funny. exciting. informative. tense. dramatic.	

28. Schools (Frequency adverbs)

Can you match these words to their approximate percentage?

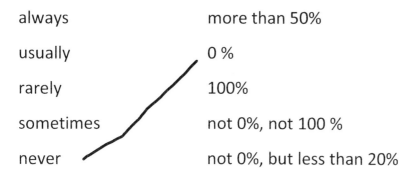

always	more than 50%
usually	0 %
rarely	100%
sometimes	not 0%, not 100 %
never	not 0%, but less than 20%

We call these words "frequency adverbs". Other examples:

- normally, generally (the same as 'usually')
- often (the opposite of 'rarely'!)

Education vocabulary

A teacher works in a school, college or university.

A student studies in a school, college or university.

In Primary Schools, we call the students "pupils". Primary Schools are for children between the ages of 5 and 11 (see the text below). Secondary Schools are for pupils/students between the ages of 11 and 16.

A college is often used to describe a place for education after the age of 16.

From the age of 18, some students study in a university.

Education in Britain: Primary Schools

In the UK, children normally start school at the age of five, but often they can start before then if the local school allows it. The school year starts in September. The youngest children generally go into a class called 'reception', then start Year 1 the following September. They stay in Primary school until Year 6. Sometimes Years 1 and 2 are called 'Infants' and Years 3-6 are called 'Juniors'. English schools usually have a school uniform. You never have to pay to go to Primary School, but some families choose a private school if they have the money and think that a private school would be better for their children. In private schools the classes are nearly always smaller than in state schools.

Can you make some sentences about schools in your country?

In my country, children start school at the age of _____.

This school is called _____.

They stay in this school until the age of _____.

Some children go to _____ (school) at the age of _____.

Frequency adverbs

Find these words in the text about *Primary Schools*:

always, often, sometimes, usually, normally, generally, never

Where did the word come in the sentence?

Sometimes we start a sentence with one of these words, but we usually place them just before the verb.

Put one of the frequency adverbs into the sentences below about your daily routine:

     I get up at 8 o'clock.

     I have breakfast.

     I play football/go for a walk in the morning.

     We have lunch at about 1 o'clock.

     In the afternoon I stay in my room or I meet some friends.

     In the evening I watch TV.

     I go to bed before nine o'clock!

29. Nice to meet you!

Read this conversation with a partner, then change the details to talk about yourself!

Person 1: Hello! What's your name?

Person 2: I'm Ludmila. And you?

P1: My name is Sabrina. Nice to meet you!

P2: It's nice to meet you too! Where do you come from?

P1: I'm from South America – and you?

P2: I'm from Moldova.

P1: Where's that?

P2: It's a small country in Europe, between Romania and Ukraine.

P1: Where do you live now?

P2: I live in the town centre. My apartment is above a shop. Do you know the Post Office? It's near there. And you – where do you live?

P1: Actually I live in a hotel at the moment.

P2: In the town centre?

P1: No, it's about three miles out of town. Tell me about yourself: what do you do in your free time?

P2: I don't have a lot of free time. I have two children, and when they are at school I need to go shopping, do the housework. I want to find a job too, so I have to look at adverts, fill in applications, that sort of thing. What about you – Do you have any family here?

P1: Not really. I have a brother, he lives in Birmingham, and he has a wife and a child, but it's just me here. How old are your children?

P2: My daughter is nine and my son is seven. So what do you like doing in your free time?

P1: I watch TV, sometimes I play games with friends at the hotel. I like meeting people, I would like to go out more, but I don't have a lot of money.

P2: Do you see your brother often?

P1: No. He doesn't have much money either, and public transport costs a lot…

*Practise this: stress the words in **bold type**:*

(First person): **Nice** to **meet** you!

(Second person): Nice to meet **you too**!

When you meet a person another time:

(First Person): **Nice** to **see** you a**gain**!

(Second person): Nice to see **you** again!

A survey

Ask these questions to at least six people!

> What is your name?
>
> Where do you live?
>
> Do you have any brothers or sisters?
>
> Do you have a job?
>
> What do you do in your free time?

Then talk (or write) about some of the people you have interviewed: here is an example…

> *This is Karen. She lives in Coventry. She has a brother but she doesn't have any sisters. She has a job in a warehouse. In her free time she watches TV and goes out with friends.*

Family words – a matching game

Can you match the words on the left with the phrases on the right?

sister	1. The woman you married!
brother	2. The wife of your brother
sister-in-law	3. the husband/ partner of your mother
husband	4. the husband of your daughter
wife	5. a female sibling
mother-in-law	6. the wife/partner of your father
father-in-law	7. the children of your son/daughter
son-in-law	8. the mother of your mother/father
stepfather	9. a male sibling
stepmother	10. a word for a brother or a sister
uncle	11. the sister of your father or mother
aunt	12. the man you married!
cousin	13. the father of your wife or husband
grandparents	14. the brother of your mother or father
grandmother	15. mother and father of your mother or father
granddaughter	16. a child of your aunt or uncle
grandchildren	17. a female child of your son or daughter
sibling	18. the mother of your husband

30. Review: Present simple tense

For most verbs, the present simple tense is easy – just say the verb! The only change is that we add -s when you speak about another person (he/she) or thing (it):

> I **live** in a hotel. I have a brother – he **lives** in Birmingham. Public transport **costs** a lot

The verb 'have' is unusual...

> I **have** a brother. He **has** a wife and a child.

...and the verb 'to be' has three spellings:

> I **am**, you **are**, we **are**, they **are**, he/she/it **is**

Negatives and questions

For most verbs, you make questions and negatives with do/does:

> Where do you live?
>
> I don't have much money
>
> He doesn't have much money either.

With 'to be', there is no 'do/does'

> What is your name? How old are your children? I am not married.

Complete the text with a suitable verb

> My name __1.___ Conrad. I ___2.___ from Lebanon. It's a small country in the Middle East. I ___3.___ married and my wife also __4.___ here. We __5.____ not have any children. I work in a shop but my wife ___6.____ not work at the moment. In my free time I ____7.____ football, but I ____8.____ not play in a team. I would like to try golf, but it ____9.____ a lot of money. And you? What ___10.____ you like doing in your free time?

31. What will the weather be like tomorrow?

Imagine the boxes on the right are a map of a country. Draw symbols to match the description you read or hear ...

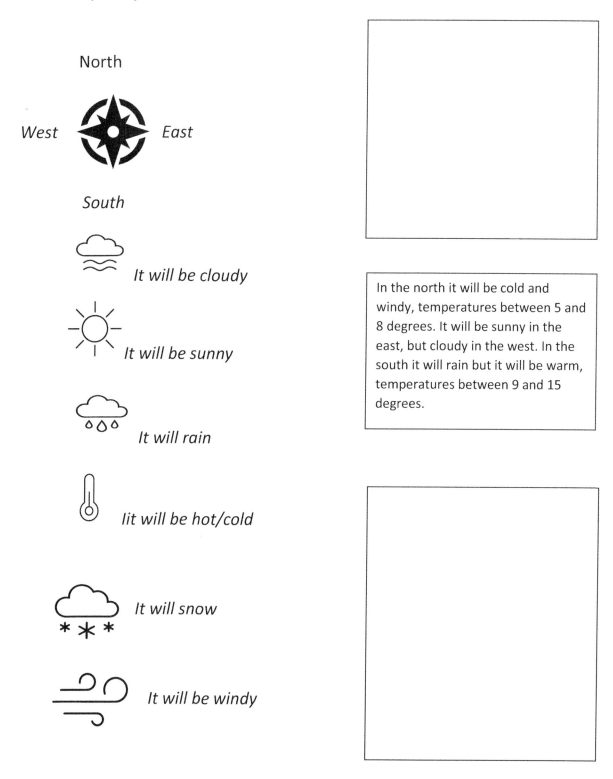

North

West   East

South

It will be cloudy

It will be sunny

It will rain

Iit will be hot/cold

It will snow

It will be windy

In the north it will be cold and windy, temperatures between 5 and 8 degrees. It will be sunny in the east, but cloudy in the west. In the south it will rain but it will be warm, temperatures between 9 and 15 degrees.

32. Taking the bus:

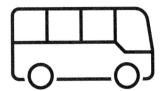

Passenger: Good morning. I want to go to Coventry, please. How much is it?

Driver: Single or return?

Passenger: Return, please.

Driver: Your best option is a Gold Day Rider ticket

Passenger: Sorry, Can you repeat that, please?

Driver: You want a Gold Day Rider ticket

Passenger: I see. How much is that?

Driver: £9.60

Passenger: And can I use this ticket to return to Rugby?

Driver: Yes

Passenger: OK. So, here's £10

Driver: 40 pence change

Passenger: Thank you. Do you stop near the cathedral?

Driver: Yes, the bus station is near the cathedral

Passenger: Thank you very much

Practise the conversation (but change the details of destination and price)

Practise the stress:

Sorry, Can you rep**eat th**at, pl**ea**se?

33. Festivals

Christmas

Probably the most important festival in England is Christmas, celebrated on the 25th December. Below are some traditions mentioned in your teacher's presentation* – circle them as you hear them mentioned.

Be careful - There are two of them that are not traditional celebrations in England!

People hang decorations in their houses

We decorate Christmas trees

We eat a big lunch of turkey and vegetables

There are special songs called Carols

People hang up a stocking by their chimney

We let off fireworks in the evening

It is an important Christian festival, celebrating the birth of Jesus Christ

We send greetings cards to friends

There is a special Christmas cake

Children put a shoe or boot outside their door on the 5th December,

and the next morning it is filled with sweets!

Another Christmas delicacy is a Mince Pie

People give each other presents

Father Christmas (or Santa Claus) gives children presents

Two more festivals:

(There is quite a lot of new vocabulary here – you will probably want to use a dictionary for some words!)

Diwali – a religious festival

Diwali is also known as the festival of lights. Originally a Hindu festival, it is now also celebrated by Sikhs and Jains. The lights symbolise the victory of light over darkness, of good over evil, and of wisdom over ignorance. It takes place between mid-October and mid-November and lasts for five days. People wear their best clothes, there are family feasts and sometimes presents are exchanged.

The Fifth of November – a historical festival

Much of Europe became Protestant during the 16th century, but some countries (e.g. France, Spain and Italy) remained Roman Catholic. Under Queen Elizabeth I, Britain had become a Protestant country. Guy Fawkes was a Catholic who wanted to overthrow King James I to replace him with a Catholic king.

On November 5th 1605 the plot to blow up (= by explosion) the Parliament building in London was discovered. Guy Fawkes was arrested. The other plotters waited at the Lion Inn in Dunchurch. When the plot failed, they fled.

Today we commemorate the failure of the plot with fireworks. Sometimes a model of Guy Fawkes is burnt on a bonfire.

What is the most important festival in your country?

When is it?

What do people do?

What do they eat?

What do they wear?

Talk about a festival in your country using the table on the next page. When you are confident, cover up parts of the table and say it again until you can say it all looking only at the key words on the right.

We have	a festival	called _____	NAME
It takes place	every year	in April	WHEN?
There is	a parade	in the city centre	PARADE
There are	fireworks	in the evening	FIREWORKS
We eat	_____	with friends/family	EAT
We drink	_____		DRINK
It lasts	for about 3 hours / 1 day/ 2 days / a week/ a month…		DURATION

Negatives:

With "There is/There are", do the same as describing places – make a negative sentence with "no":

There are no fireworks and no parades.

With a verb (like "eat" or "drink") remember to use "do not":

In Ramadan we do not eat during the day.

We do not drink alcohol.

We do not wear any special clothes.

*Teacher's presentation on Christmas**

Christmas is an important Christian festival, celebrating the birth of Christ. Some people will go to church, and in the weeks before Christmas there are special services featuring the traditional Christmas songs, called 'Carols'. Most people enjoy the festival for its traditional food, and for exchanging presents. The food includes the Christmas dinner, normally eaten at lunchtime on the 25th of December, usually turkey and vegetables followed by Christmas Pudding. There is also a traditional Christmas cake, and a lighter delicacy called 'mince pies'. People send cards to friends and family, and give presents to those closest to them. Sometimes the children are told that their presents come from Father Christmas, or Santa Claus, who is supposed to come down the chimney on Christmas Eve (the night before Christmas). Children hang up a stocking near the fireplace for him to fill with presents. Houses are decorated and families put a Christmas Tree in a prominent place in the house. They decorate the tree with lights and small hanging decorations. Sometimes people even decorate the outside of their house with lights.

34. What do you wear?

Read the text:

In summer, I usually wear a T-shirt and trousers or shorts. I sometimes wear a jumper if it's not very warm. When I go out, I often wear a jacket. If it's hot, I wear sandals.

In winter, I wear a jumper or a sweatshirt, a shirt and trousers – mostly jeans. If I want to dress smartly, I have a suit, but I rarely wear it. When I go out, I put on a warm coat.

My wife usually wears trousers and a top. She sometimes wears a dress, but she never wears skirts. She often wears sandals.

We prefer wearing casual clothes, but sometimes it's nice to wear something smart. What about you? What do you like wearing?

Do you like drawing? Your teacher will show you some clothes (or draw them). Draw the clothes in the boxes!

Casual clothes:

a top	a T-shirt	trousers
shorts	a jumper	sandals

Smart clothes:

a suit	a jacket	a shirt
a dress	a skirt	a coat

Now answer the question "What do you like wearing?"

Use words like "sometimes"/"usually"/ "rarely" in your sentences. (Can you remember where to put these words in a sentence? Check Unit 28 on "Schools (frequency adverbs)".)

Say some sentences to a partner starting with these words…

In summer I usually wear…

In winter …

If I want to be smart, I wear …

If it's very cold, …

I rarely wear …

Shopping for clothes

Read this conversation:

- Can I help you?

- Certainly, … How do they feel?

- Take them off and I'll go and look for a bigger size. What size are you?

- We have these – they are not quite the same but in your size.

- They are £36. The other ones were in the sale, but these are full price.

- *Yes please. I like these sandals – can I try them on?*

- *They are a bit small.*

- *I'm not sure. Just a bit bigger than these please.*

- *Yes, they are much better. How much are they?*

- *Oh, I see. I'll leave it for now, thank you.*

35. A conversation about the weather

Read the conversation with a partner two or three times: each time change the *weather phrases* to something different!

A: Hello. How are you?

B: Not bad, thanks, and you?

A: Fine! *It's a nice day.*

B: Yes. Do you have any plans?

A: No, nothing special. Tomorrow we want to go to Birmingham.

B: What will the weather be like tomorrow?

A: On the BBC they say *it will rain* in the morning but *there will be sunny spells* in the afternoon.

B: I see. I hope you have a nice day. Next weekend they say *it will be hot and sunny*.

A: What are you doing at the weekend?

B: I don't know yet.

A: I have to go. I have an appointment.

B: Nice to see you. Take care!

A: You too! Bye!

36. When we use "the"

(The definite article)

Read this text:

> There is a shopping mall in Rugby. The mall is called 'Rugby Central'. It is not very big – there are about 30 shops. The shops are quite small, but there are a few bigger ones. Near the mall there is a market on Fridays and Saturdays. You can buy a lot of things at the market – fruit, vegetables, even clothes.

Normally the first time you talk about something, you say 'a'*

There is a shopping mall… there is a market…

*('an' before a vowel: *There is an interesting museum*)

When you talk about it again, use 'the'. We use 'the' when we know what is talked about.

We can use 'the' with singular or plural, but you can only use 'a' (or 'an') before a singular. The first time you mention something in the plural, you can use a number, the word 'some', or nothing!

There are shops, some banks, and three churches in the town centre.

Try to complete this text with 'a', 'an', 'the' (or nothing!)

Welcome to the hotel. There are 90 ___ rooms. ___ rooms all have en-suite bathrooms. There is ___ restaurant on the ground floor. You will find ___ restaurant to the right of reception. There is ___ fitness room, and on Saturday there is ___ aerobics class in ___ fitness room at 11 am. There are ___ toilets on the ground floor next to ___ restaurant.

Describe a place you know – a town, or a building.

37. Regular past tense verbs

For regular verbs, you add **-ed** to the present simple verb.

For example: play (present simple) = play**ed** (past simple)

Pronunciation: After 'd' or 't' add an extra syllable: e.g. "waited" (sounds like "way-tid")

For regular verbs, the **-ed** ending is for all persons – I played, he played, you played, we played, they played…

Present	Past
watch	watched
clean	
listen	
wash	
work	
phone	
talk	
stay	

Write a suitable verb in the past simple tense to complete this text:

Yesterday I _____ at home. I _____ my room in the morning. I _____ to music, and I _____ a friend. I _____ to him for 20 minutes. In the afternoon I _____ football, and I _____ some clothes. In the evening I _____ a film on TV.

38. The weather tomorrow and yesterday

First, here is another set of details about the weather tomorrow, as in Unit 31:

North

West East

South

It will be cloudy

It will be sunny

In the north there will be showers, temperatures will be cold, between 5 and 8 degrees. It will be cloudy in the east, but sunny in the west. In the south there will be sunny spells and it will be warm, temperatures between 9 and 15 degrees.

It will rain

it will be hot/cold

It will snow

It will be windy

Past, and future!

Now you can describe the weather yesterday and tomorrow!

'is' → 'was' in the past simple tense

yesterday		tomorrow
it was sunny.		it will be sunny
it rained		it will rain.

Practise talking about your activities: choose from these verbs:

stay	play	watch	walk	talk
phone	clean	work	listen	wash

Example: Yesterday I stayed at home. I watched a film in the evening. Tomorrow I will clean my room and wash some clothes.

Remember you need 'do' for questions and negative sentences ('did' in the past).

Yesterday I did not play tennis because it was cold. Tomorrow I will not work.

What did you do yesterday?

What will you do tomorrow?

39. Conversation: At the café/restaurant

You have a new job as a waiter/a waitress in a café! Practise the conversation in groups of three. You can change the words in brackets with something different from the menu.

Starters	Main courses	Desserts	Drinks
Tomato soup	Lasagne	Cheesecake	Tea
Vegetable soup	Chicken pie	Sticky toffee	Filter coffee
Goat's cheese tart	Fish and chips	pudding	Coca-Cola
Avocado	Cottage Pie	Ice cream (vanilla,	Lemonade
Sweet chili prawns	Mushroom risotto	chocolate,	Orange
		strawberry)	juice

Waiter/waitress: Are you ready to order?

Customer 1: Yes please. I'd like (tomato soup) to start.

Customer 2: And I'll have the (goat's cheese tart) please

Waiter/waitress: Certainly. And to follow?

Customer 1: I'll have the (fish and chips) please

Customer 2: What vegetables are there with the (chicken pie?)

Waiter/waitress: I think it is with peas and chips

Customer 2: Actually I think I'll have the (mushroom risotto)

Waiter/Waitress: So that's (*repeat the order to check*). Anything to drink?

Customer 2: Yes please. I'll have (an orange juice)

Customer 1: I'll have (water), please

* * * * * * * * * * * * * *

Waiter/waitress: Was everything OK for you?

Customer 2: Yes, thank you

Waiter/Waitress: Can I get you a dessert?

(*Finish the conversation, order desserts, teas or coffees... at the end one of the customers asks "Can we have the bill please?"*)

40. Uncountable nouns

English nouns can be **countable** or **uncountable.**

Countable nouns can be counted! – 1 brother, 2 brothers, 3 brothers...

They can be singular – in this case they can have 'a' (or 'an' before a vowel):

> *There is an airport in Birmingham.*

> *I have a friend in London.*

They normally take '-s' in the plural:

> *There are shops, cafés and 3 schools in my town.*

> *I have a brother and two sisters.*

('Children' is an unusual plural: one child, two children, three children...)

Uncountable nouns cannot be counted – they are always singular:

You cannot say "~~2 informations~~"

We never use 'a' or 'an' with uncountable nouns (~~an information~~ is incorrect)

We often use the word 'some' ('any' in questions and negatives) with uncountable nouns:

> Would you like some food? Do you have any cash?

Examples of uncountable nouns:

- concepts e.g. **money, cash, happiness, information, knowledge, travel, work**

- group nouns e.g. **furniture, accommodation, baggage, traffic**

- substances e.g. many food words – **food, rice, pasta, cheese*, meat**

- school subjects e.g. **history, maths, English, art, music...**

Sometimes a word can be both countable and uncountable!

We are a bit flexible with words like 'cheese'* - It is normally uncountable but you will sometimes see/hear 'cheeses' – *There are many cheeses for sale in our supermarket.* It is better to say *There are many types of cheese...*

'a chicken, 2 chickens, 3 chickens...' (countable) describes the animals in the farmyard, but in a restaurant we use chicken as an uncountable noun.

I would like chicken and chips, please.

Take a piece of paper and write the headings 'countable' or 'uncountable' at the top of two columns...

Countable	Uncountable

Write these words in the correct column. Are there any that you could put in both columns?

advice, cake, furniture, museum, economics, road, computer, tennis, shop, cat, child, lesson, kindness, sister, car, chemistry, engineering, cup, fork, money...

Differences in the way we use countable and uncountable nouns:

countable	uncountable
Can be singular or plural	Always singular
Can have 'a' (or 'an')	Cannot have 'a' (or 'an') – use 'some' or 'any' if necessary
How many + plural	How much
A few + plural	A little

Both types of noun can be used with 'the'

You can also use the word 'some' with a countable noun in the plural or an uncountable noun (or 'any' in a question or negative).

Try this exercise: choose from the box below to complete this text of a conversation in a village shop, but be careful! For two of the answers, it is best to have nothing!

Shop assistant: Good morning! What would you like?

Customer: I would like ___1.___ cheese, please.

Shop assistant: Certainly – it is in ___2.___ fridge behind you.

Customer: Do you have ___3___ bananas?

Shop assistant: Sorry, not today. We will have ___4.___ delivery of ___5___ fruit tomorrow.

Customer: I see. How ___6.___ is the cheese?

Shop assistant: Three pounds, please.

Customer: Oh, that's a lot of ___7___ money.

Shop assistant: There is ___8___ smaller packet there. It's only One pound fifty

Customer: Thank you. I will take the small packet. I would also like __9___ apples.

Shop assistant: How ___10___ would you like?

Customer: Three please.

Shop assistant : Here you are. That's two pounds eighty, please.

a	an	some	any	much	many	(or nothing!)

When you have finished, practise reading the conversation with a partner.

41. Kitchen equipment

Cutlery:

a knife and a fork    a spoon

a teaspoon

Crockery:

a cup and saucer    a mug

a plate   (a dinner plate, a tea plate...)

a dish/a bowl

What word fits in the space?

A _____ of sugar

A _____ of coffee

A _____ of rice

A _____ of tea

Practise the words by asking: "Can I have a _____ , please?"

Countable or uncountable?

sugar, coffee, rice and *tea* are all uncountable (substance words).

All the kitchen words above used with 'a' are countable: *a teaspoon, 2 teaspoons, 3 teaspoons* etc.

The words *crockery* and *cutlery* are uncountable (group nouns).

A cup of/ a plate of/ a bowl of can be used with countable words in the plural:

A plate of beans, a bowl of corn flakes, a cup of blueberries.

Activity to do at home:

Look at a simple recipe (the instructions for cooking something) and read the list of ingredients: ask yourself if the food words are countable or uncountable. Here is an example:

Little Cakes

You will need:

    2   eggs

    100 grams (4 ounces) of soft margarine

    100 grams (4 ounces) of caster sugar

    100 grams (4 ounces) of self-raising flour

    6 glacé cherries

    (*This is from a recipe book for children – you may find a children's recipe is easier to understand!*)

    Countable: *egg, gram, ounce, cherry*

    Uncountable: *margarine, sugar, flour*

42. Questions: Who am I?

Your teacher will choose a famous person (some examples below). Ask questions to find the person! Your teacher can only answer "yes" or "no"!

Are you	a man/ a woman?
Do you live in	Europe/Africa/ Asia/America/The Middle East?
Do you come from	Europe/Africa/ Asia/America/The Middle East?
Are you	young/middle-aged/old?
Are you	a politician/ a musician/ an actor/ a sports person?/ a religious person/ a TV personality?
Are you	popular/funny/good-looking?
Do you play	football/tennis/basketball?
Do you play	the piano/the guitar/a musical instrument?
Do you wear	glasses?
Do you have	a beard/ black hair/blond hair/ brown hair/ white hair?
Some ideas:	*Beyoncé Mo Salah Elton John Tom Cruise*
	Christiano Ronaldo Joe Biden Rafael Nadal
	The pope Paul McCartney Novak Djokovic
	King Charles The Prime Minister

Question words: To ask more interesting questions, you will need:

Where …?	(The answer is a place)
What…?	(The answer is a thing or an activity)
Who…?	(The answer is a person)
How…?	(The answer explains a method)
How much?	(The answer is a price)
How many?	(The answer is a quantity)
How old…?	(The answer is an age)
Why…?	(The answer is a reason)
When…?	(The answer is a point in time e.g. a day, a date, a time of day)

Questionnaire: Ask at least three people and note your answers on the grid

	Person 1	Person 2	Person 3
Name			
Origin			
Address			
Activity?			
Free time			
Sport?			
Music?			

Now speak (or write about the person: Here is an example

His/Her name is (Jane). He/She comes from London, but now he/she lives in Rugby. He/She is an engineer, but he/she is retired now. In his/her free time she likes reading and watching films. He/She plays badminton and he/she likes music, but he/she does not play an instrument.

_____

_____

_____

_____

Here is the answer – what is the question?!

Example: Answer -"Monday"

The question could be: *When do you have an English lesson?*

Answer - "I like playing tennis"

The question could be: *What sports do you like? Or What do you do in your free time?*

Answer – "Three pounds 50"

The question could be: *"How much is it (to go to Coventry)?"*

43. Countries (2)

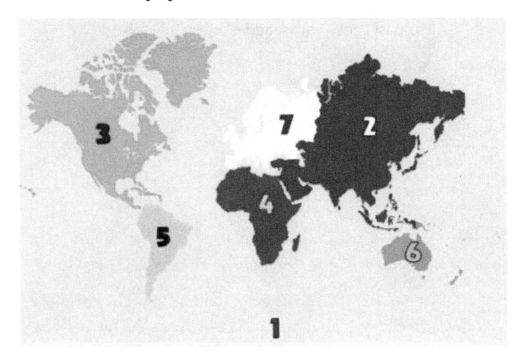

Which number is which continent?

Antarctica............. *1*

Europe................. __

Africa.................. __

Asia..................... __

North America.... __

South America.... __

Oceania.............. __

Which continent are these countries in? Work with a partner...

Argentina, Australia, Belgium, Canada, China, Ethiopia, France, Gabon, India, Kazakhstan, Libya, Nigeria, Peru, Poland, Russia, Sudan, Switzerland, the USA

Some areas are not shown on the map: Which countries are in...?

- The Middle East

- Central America

44. The past tense: Irregular verbs

Reminder: regular past tense verbs: add – ed to the verb

I played football yesterday. I scored a goal!

Questions and negatives in the past: we use 'did' (not) + verb

Did you have a nice weekend? Not really – I did not (or 'didn't) do much.

"am/is" in the present -> was

"are" in the present -> were

Some other verbs have irregular spellings. Here are some important ones:

Verb	Past simple tense
have	had
go	went
(be)come	(be)came
speak	spoke
eat	ate
drink	drank
sleep	slept
(under)stand	(under)stood
lose	lost
get	got
forget	forgot
give	gave
know	knew
read	read [*pronounced like 'red'*]
tell	told
say	said [*pronounced sed*]
send	sent
leave	left
hear	heard
see	saw

Remember: if it is a question or a negative, use 'did' + verb (even for irregular verbs) e.g. I did not have any lunch. Did you see the film yesterday?

Fill in the gaps with the right form of the verbs in brackets.

I _____ (have) a nice day yesterday. I _____ (get) up early and _____ (go) to the station. I _____ (visit) some family in Birmingham. We _____ (speak) about many things, we _____ (have) a good lunch, and we _____ (drink) a lot! In the afternoon we _____ (see) a film, but I _____ (sleep) for some time and I did not _____ (see) the end of the film. I _____ (leave) at about 6 o'clock and _____ (come) back here. I ____ not have any dinner because I ___ (be) not hungry. I _____ (go) to bed at ten o'clock.

Birmingham City Hall

45. Times

Say these times digitally e.g. 2.10 = two ten

- 1.20

- 3.35

- 6.30

- 10.45

- 11.00

- (if you have a time with __.00, say "o'clock")

Two ways of saying times:

• 11.30 = Eleven thirty	• Half past eleven
• 8.15 = eight fifteen	• A quarter past eight
• 7.45 = seven forty-five	• A quarter to eight
• 5.20 = five twenty	• Twenty past five
• 1.30 = one thirty	• Half past one
• 2.40 = two forty	• Twenty to three
• 4.50 = four fifty	• Ten to five

Write digitally the time you hear e.g. if you hear "twenty to four" you write "3.40"

- *Practise saying times in pairs: say the time in one way, then the other person says the alternative way*

- The twenty-four hour clock: For bus times, train times, plane times and some official events you will hear times like "14.28" = fourteen twenty-eight. For "20.00" you sometimes hear twenty hundred hours. This is rare in normal conversation: if we need to be clear if it is morning or evening, we say "am" (before 12 noon) or "pm" (after noon)

- We never use "past" or "to" with times over 13 (so we never say "ten past fourteen")

46. My day

Read the text about Gina's day:

"I get up at six fifty on the days when I work. I have a shower and get dressed. I have breakfast between quarter past seven and half past seven, and I leave the house at twenty to eight. I meet a friend at the bus stop and we go together to work. I start work at eight forty-five, and I finish at half past four. In the evening I do my housework and go to bed at about ten o'clock.

At the weekend I get up later – at about eight thirty. Sometimes I go for a walk or a bike ride. I try to meet friends on Saturday evening. I go to bed at about midnight!"

Say the times of your normal daily routine. Use the time expressions (half past, quarter to etc.) for some times, but it always OK to use the digital version.

During the week I normally get up at (half past seven).

I have breakfast between eight o'clock and eight fifteen...

...

I usually go to bed at about a quarter past ten, but if it is the weekend I go to bed later. On Saturday and Sunday I get up .....

47. Villages, towns, cities (Part 1)

Rugby

1. Listen to a presentation* about the town of Rugby and put the missing words/numbers in the right place.

Rugby is a town in _____. It was a small town until the _____ century. The famous Rugby School was started in _____. The sport of Rugby started at the school in _____ when a boy picked up the ball and ran with it! The town became more important with the development of the _____. Today the _____ of Rugby is about _____ (eighty thousand). It is a pleasant town. There is a market on Fridays and Saturdays.

(*Teachers can read the presentation at the end of the next section).

1567	population	railway	80000	nineteenth	1823	Warwickshire

Read the text about Rugby to another person when you are ready!

More vocabulary of places:

a castle   a palace   a town hall   a parliament building

a swimming pool   a sports centre   a theatre   a cinema

a lake   a museum   an art gallery   a bus station

Use the words to talk about your village/town/city – if the place does not have something, say the sentence in the negative:

There are no art galleries, there are no theatres, but there is a museum.

Useful adjectives (describing words):

beautiful   old   new   interesting   important

big   small   ancient   useful   famous   excellent

48. Villages, towns, cities (Part 2)

Read the text about Coventry:

Coventry is a city in the West Midlands, England.

Coventry had a population of 316,915 at the 2011 census making it the 11th largest city in the United Kingdom.

It is 19 miles (31 km) east of Birmingham, and 95 miles (153 km) north-west of London.

The modern Coventry Cathedral was built after the 14th-century cathedral church of Saint Michael was destroyed in 1940 during the second world war. Coventry motor companies have contributed significantly to the British motor industry, and there is a transport museum in the city centre. The shopping centre has all major shops and a covered market. There is an airport, but it is not very big. The city has three universities: Coventry University, the University of Warwick on the southern outskirts and the smaller private Arden University close to Coventry Airport.

Dunchurch, Rugby and Coventry

Use the table below to make sentences about Dunchurch, Rugby and Coventry

It is	a village	a town	a city
The population is	about 3000	about 80,000	about 300,000
There is	a fine church	a famous school	a cathedral
There are	a few shops	a lot of shops	all major shops
There is also	an old pub	an important railway station	a transport museum
It is	3 miles south of Rugby	12 miles east of Coventry	19 miles east of Birmingham

Can you remember...

... some sentences about a town or city that you know

The town (or city) is called _____

There is a castle/ a museum/ a station/a primary school	There is...
There are parliament buildings/shops/cafés/schools	There are...
There are no churches/mosques/ temples/schools/shops	There are no...
It has a station/ an airport	It has...
It doesn't have a station/an airport	It doesn't have...

Teacher's presentation about the town of Rugby:

Rugby is a medium-sized town in the county of Warwickshire. In fact it was just a small town until the nineteenth century. The main feature of the small town was its famous school, which was founded in 1567. It was here at the school that the sport of Rugby started in 1823, when a boy called William Webb Ellis picked up a football and started to run with it. The town grew with the development of the railways, and it is still an important junction for the railway network. To day the population is about eighty thousand. It is a pleasant town with many facilities, and it is not far from the city of Coventry.

49. Revision: the weather / modal verbs

Write the weather forecast:

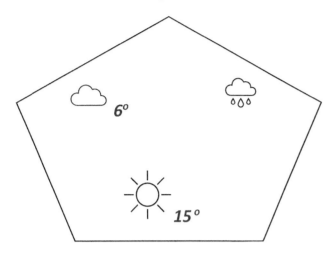

In the north-east it will _____. In the north-west it ____ ____ cold – the

temperature ____ be ____ and it _____ ____ cloudy. In the south ___ ____ ___

_____ and the temperature ____ _____ _____.

Have a conversation:

- *It's a nice day!/It's not a very nice day*
- *What's the weather forecast for tomorrow?*
- *On the BBC, they say it will...*

Modal Verbs (used with another verb)

can	able to e.g. I can speak French but I can't speak Spanish
will*	Future e.g. Tomorrow I will go swimming.
may	Permission e.g. May I sit here?
must	Obligation e.g. I must (I have to) pass a test.
could	Polite 'can' e.g. Could you write that down for me, please? (also 'can' in the past e.g. I could not understand the film.)
would like	Want (but more polite) e.g. Would you like a cup of tea?

*Sometimes "shall" is used instead of will

Using the verbs you have seen, practise the modal verbs:

walk   listen   watch   cook   sleep
meet my friends   drink   eat   read
swim   clean   shop   speak

Write five things you will do tomorrow:

1. Tomorrow I will _____
2. I will _____
3. I _____
4. Also, _____
5. and _____

Now write two things you can do, and one thing you can't do:

I can_____ and I can_____, but I can't_____

Now two things you must do:

I must _____ and _____

Finally, write something to finish these sentences:

I would like to_____

May I _____ ?

Could you _____, please?

50. A journey

Complete the text with the words from the box.

Last Saturday I _____(1) to Coventry by bus. I _____ (2) Rugby after breakfast with a friend. We _____ (3) for the bus for ten minutes, then the journey _____ (4) about fifty minutes. We _____ (5) in Coventry at 11.00 o'clock. We _____ (6) the shopping centre in the centre of the city, and we _____(7) a sandwich from Greggs. My friend also _____(8) a coffee. We did not _____(9) any clothes because they _____(10) too expensive. We _____(11) to Rugby at the end of the afternoon. It _____(12) not take long – less than an hour.

do/did	was/were	go/went	buy/bought
arrive/arrived	leave/left	take/took	wait/waited
visit/visited	have/had	return/returned	

by bus

by car   by boat

by train   by plane

Describe a journey, for example your journey to where you are now.

I came to (Rugby) by (car). Before I was in (Worcester). The journey did not take long/took a long time. I left (Worcester) at 10.00 o'clock in the morning, and I arrived here (one hour) later.

_____

_____

_____

_____

51. What are you doing?

Present Continuous tense

The present-continuous tense (sometimes called the 'Present Progressive' tense) talks about what we are doing **at the moment, right now.**

We make this by adding the verb 'to be' (am/is/are), and then adding -ing to the verb.

*e.g. I **am** play**ing** football at the moment.*

*I **am** learn**ing** English.*

*You **are** eat**ing** chicken.*

*He **is** walk**ing** to school.*

*They **are** speak**ing** Arabic.*

With weather verbs e.g. "rain", we can use the Present Continuous

What's the weather like? It's raining, but it's not too cold.

Look out of the window! It's snowing!

It is also used for the very near future, e.g.

What are you doing this weekend? I am going to see a friend.

Find examples of the present continuous in this phone conversation, then read the conversation with a partner:

Person 1 (Gina): Hello?
Person 2 (Claire): Hi Gina, it's Claire. What are you doing at the moment?
Gina: Nothing much. I'm cooking dinner. Why?
Claire: Is it OK if I drop by with some clothes for the children? I'm going into town and I could stop by at your place on the way.

Gina: Yes, of course. I'm not going out.
Claire: Great. I will be there in about twenty minutes.
Gina: What are you doing in town?
Claire: I'm picking up my daughter. She's playing at a friend's house this afternoon.
Gina: OK. I'll see you soon. Bye!
Claire: Bye!

Write the correct present continuous sentence

1. My friend _____ (visit) me.
2. I _____ (listen) to music.
3. Mary _____ (watch) TV.
4. Farah_____ (clean) his room.
5. My children _____ (go) to the cinema with a friend.

Speak about what you are wearing today:

I am wearing….

Close your eyes and try to remember what the person next to you is wearing!

You are wearing …

Warning: Don't use this tense too much! It is useful mainly if the other person cannot see something e.g. when you are on the phone

- *Hi ! What are you doing at the moment?*
- *Nothing much. I'm watching television.*

52. Prepositions

Words used with a noun (or proper noun), often to describe position (**in, on, at, over, under, next to*, behind, in front of*, near, opposite...**).

Other common prepositions include:

to, about, for, by, with, of, from, out of*, before, after, until, between, in spite of* ...

(*You can see that some prepositions have more than one word.)

Prepositions are small (but important!) words!

The most common prepositions are **in, on** and **to**.

Where is your son? He's **in** the garden.

Last weekend I went to Coventry. I went **to** the shops and **to** the Transport Museum.

Where is my phone? I think it's **on** the table **in** the kitchen.

*Try describing where things or people are in a picture. You may also need **next to**, or **between**.*

The bank is **next to** the cinema, **between** the cinema and a baker's shop.

  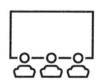

Time phrases

- We use **on** with days of the week: **On** Monday, **On** Saturday...
- We use **at** with times of the clock: My English lesson is **at** 10 o'clock.
- We use **in** with periods of time such as morning, afternoon and evening, months, seasons and years: **in** the morning, **in** August, **in** summer, **in** 2016...

Look at a text and identify the prepositions.

Can you complete this conversation with the right prepositions?

- *- What do you do _(1)__ Saturdays?*

- *- Well, __(2)_ the morning I don't do very much. I get up __(3)_ 8.30. Normally _(4)__ the afternoon I go out with friends, but I get back _(5)__ my house for dinner _(6)__ 6.30 _(7)__ the evening. And you?*

- *- I go swimming _(8)__ 9.00 o'clock _(10)__ Saturday morning. There is a pool _(11)__ a fitness centre near my home. It's __(12)___ the town centre and the cement factory. __(13)__ the afternoon I sometimes go shopping _(14)__ the retail park.*

(Did you have any problems with number 12? Try 'between'!)

Some more examples:

In spite of the bad weather, we had a nice time **on** holiday.

We stayed in town **until** six o'clock. **By** then, the restaurants were open.

This is a book **about** life in the nineteenth century **by** the famous author, Charles Dickens .

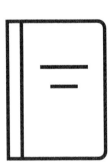

53. Secondary schools

Subjects in secondary school include:

English (often the study of English Literature)   **Maths**

Sciences (Physics, Biology and Chemistry)

Technology (sometimes called "D and T" – design and technology)

Information Technology/Computing   **a Modern Foreign Language**

History   **Geography**   **Religious Education**

Art   **Music**   **Physical Education (P.E.)**   **Drama**

Listen to the presentation* about secondary schools and complete the sentences here. The missing words you need are in the box under the sentences, but there are some extra words that you do not need!

English children go to a secondary school at the age of _____.

Most go to a _____ school, but some pass a test to attend a _____ school.

About ____ per cent attend a private, or independent school.

At the age of _____ they take GCSEs.

GCSEs are _____ in the different subjects.

It is important to pass GCSEs in English and _____.

After that, some children stay in the same school and study for _____ examinations.

These are quite _____ and are necessary for university entrance.

Others go to a college, where they may study for A Levels or take more _____ courses.

Most children leave school at the age of _____.

six	ten	eleven	fifteen	sixteen	eighteen
Comprehensive		examinations		Grammar	GCSEs
A-Levels		vocational		academic	Maths

93

What about in your home country? Look back at the chapter about Primary schools, then talk to a partner about the education system. Here is an example:

"In my country a good education is quite expensive. There are state schools and all children go to school at the age of six, but the private schools are better because the classes in the state schools are very big. Some children leave school at the age of fourteen, but if you want to go to university you must go to a High School until the age of eighteen. The exams are called "Highers", and you need a good score in these exams to get a place at university. You have to study about eight subjects for the Highers, including Maths, Science and a Language."

(*Here is a script for the presentation about Secondary Schools in England)

At the age of eleven English children go to Secondary School, but there are several names you will hear for these – Comprehensive Schools, High Schools, Grammar Schools, Academies... Most of the state schools are "Comprehensive", which means that all children can go there, but in some towns and cities it is possible to go to a "Grammar School", which is more academic and you have to pass a test to enter these. Typically Secondary Schools will teach Maths, Sciences, English (Language and Literature), a modern foreign language, Geography, History, Art, Music, Technology (including Information Technology) and Religious Education. All children do some Physical Education (P.E.) and sometimes Drama and Dance are school subjects. In Grammar Schools and Independent (Private) Schools the pupils may also study Latin. Independent Schools are quite popular – about 8 per cent of secondary school age children go to them, even though they can be very expensive! At the age of sixteen there are important examinations called 'GCSEs'. Pupils must take GCSE in English, Science and Maths, but they may be able to choose other subjects – it depends on the school. Usually they take at least six subjects, but they may take as many as eleven. A GCSE pass in English and Maths is very important as a basic requirement for many jobs.

Some schools have a "sixth form" where the children can stay until the age of 18, but between the ages of 16 and 18 many go to a college. If a pupil wants to study at university, they normally take 'A Level' exams at the age of 18. These are quite academic, and the pupils chooses just three or four subjects. Alternatively, pupils/students do a more practical course at a college, sometimes called "vocational" courses because they prepare for a job. Most English children leave school at the age of 18.

54. Food and drink, recipes

Can you put the food and drink below into the right category?

meat	vegetable	fruit	cereals	dairy	desserts/cakes

milk   chicken   carrots   oats   apples

lamb   peas   rice   cheesecake   bananas

beans   beef   yoghurt   cheese   potatoes

oranges   pears   crumble   aubergine   tomatoes

pork   chips   rhubarb   cream   butter

- *Do you like rhubarb?*
- *I don't know, I've never tried it!*

What other food ingredients are important for you?

Describing a dish

Lasagna is a pasta dish. It comes from Italy, but it is very popular in Britain. You can buy Lasagna sheets in the supermarket – they are rectangular. The meat sauce is usually minced beef with tomatoes, onions and garlic. You fry the onions and the garlic slowly, then add the meat. When the meat is brown, add the tomatoes. You arrange the meat sauce and the lasagna sheets in layers, then pour a cheese sauce over the top and bake in the oven for about half an hour. You can buy the cheese sauce in a jar, or make it with butter, milk and a little flour, cooked in a saucepan, and mix in the cheese just before you pour it over the lasagna.

Now describe a dish you like:

It is called_____

It is made with _____, _____, _____ and _____.

You cook it in the oven/in a saucepan/ in a frying pan.

Important verbs:

mix   fry   bake   arrange   chop   pour

55. Inside a building

Describe where you live, and listen to other people describing their houses or apartments.

In my house/my apartment/my flat, there is...

...a living room

...a kitchen

...a bathroom

...an en-suite shower room

There are ...

...(2) bedrooms

It has /It doesn't have...

... a dining room

... a cellar

...a games room

...a utility room (where there is a washing machine)

...a study

Check the meanings of these words too (useful for bigger buildings):

A corridor

A staircase

A lift/an elevator

A foyer

56. Pronunciation (vowels)

Short vowel	Long vowel (as when spelling)
can	cane (same sound: *ai* – rain)
met	mete (same sound: *ee* and *ea* -meet and meat)
sit	site (same sound: *igh* – high, night, fight)
con	cone (same sound: oa – boat, roast)
tub	tube

If there are two (or more) consonants after the vowel, the short pronunciation is normal:

landed, banner, matter, …

kettle, messy, better, …

bitter, milled, kissed, …

floppy, topped, conned, …

butter, clubbed, funny,…

Two vowel combinations:

(Some of these are shown above e.g. ea and ee)

ou (normally the same with **ow**): south, down, how, out, towel, roundabout

oi: coin, moist, voice

oo: boot, tooth, root, zoo

Unfortunately, there are many exceptions to these patterns!

57. More past tense practice: Last Saturday...

Last Saturday, I _____(1) a good day. I _____ (2) until 8.30, so I did not _____(3) breakfast. I _____(4) up, _____(5) my room and _____(6) a cup of coffee. Then I _____(7) a message to a friend. We _____ (8) into town and I _____(9) a magazine. My friend _____(10) a nice jacket but it _____(11) too expensive so we did not _____ (12) it. After lunch, we _____(13) games with some children, and an English friend _____(14) to visit. He _____(15) me a book and so in the evening I _____(16) for an hour, then I _____ (17) a film in the hall. It _____(18) a film with Tom Cruise and Nicole Kidman, and I thought they _____(19) excellent. In bed, I _____(20) a puzzle before going to sleep.	have, sleep have, get, leave, drink send, go buy, see be, buy, play come, bring, read watch, be be, do

1.   2.   3.   4.   5.

6.   7.   8   9.   10.

11.   12.   13.   14.   15.

16.   17.   18.   19.   20.

(You can repeat the exercise by covering the answers)

58. Talking about your life

Listen and complete the text with the missing words (in the box below)

Peter Smith was born ___ 1978. He grew up ___ London, but his parents moved ___ the Midlands when he was twelve. He went ___ a secondary school in Coventry. When he was sixteen, he went __ a college and studied economics. After college, he was unemployed __ four months, then he had several jobs. He worked ___ a bank for a year, then he got a job ___ an insurance company. He did not like the job very much, and after three months he changed again. He worked ___ the office of a distribution company. ___2001, he left that job and trained to be an estate agent. Now he sells houses, or finds tenants ___ rented accommodation. He likes the job because he meets a lot of people and he doesn't have to sit ___his office all the time.

in	to	for

Here are some notes about Peter Smith. Use the notes to tell the story of his life

- -born in 1978

- -grew up in London

- - parents moved to the Midlands

- - went to secondary school in Coventry

- - went to college, studied economics

- - unemployed for four months

- - several jobs – bank, insurance company (☹), distribution company

- - 2001 trained as an estate agent

- - now sells houses or finds tenants for rented accommodation

- -likes his job

Your life so far!

I was born in _____ (year?)

I grew up in _____ (place)

I went to school in _____ (place) for _____ years

I moved to England in _____ (year?)

59. Daily routine

To get: a difficult verb!

1. = to receive: *I got an email from _____. Did you get any nice presents for your birthday? What kind of meals do you get here?*

I've got = I have…Have you got = Do you have?

Have you got a pen? = Do you have a pen? – Yes, I've got one here!

2. = to become: *I get tired. I get dressed. I got married in 1981*
3. There are a lot of combinations with 'get': get up/ get in/ get over/ get on/get off etc!

A typical day

(Look back at Unit 46 "My day" and read about Gina's day to revise.)

Fill in the missing words to describe a typical day:

I get _____ at about _____ . I _____ a shower and get dressed, then I go to breakfast at _____. Sometimes I _____ _____ _____ in the morning. I have lunch at _____ and in the afternoon I _____ _____ _____ _____. Dinner is at _____, and in the evening I _____ _____ or _____ _____ _____. I normally _____ to bed at _____.

Some ideas:

I **play** football/tennis/computer games/pool.

I **go** for a walk/a run.

I **read** a book.

I **watch** TV

I **talk** with friends.

I **watch** a film.

I **have** an English lesson.

Do you have children? Talk about the daily routine of a young person you know. Don't forget that you need an -s on the verb! For example:

My daughter Illa goes to Secondary School. She gets up at 6.30. She doesn't eat a lot of breakfast! She leaves the house at 7.15 and takes the bus to school. She gets home at about 4.30. In the evening she watches TV or plays games on the computer. Sometimes she has homework for school. At the weekend she gets up very late – sometimes not until 11 o'clock!

Yesterday

You will need to use the past tense for your verbs:

Present	Past
Regular: (play, watch, talk…)	-ed (played, watched, walked)
get	got
have	had
go	went
read	read [*pronounced: red*]
Negative: do not (have)	did not (have)

Write the sentences above for yesterday:

I got up at about _____. I had a shower and _____

_____

_____

_____

Have a conversation with another person in your class:

What did you do yesterday?

What time did you get up?

What did you do in the morning?

When did you have lunch/dinner?

What did you have for lunch/dinner?

What did you do in the evening?

What time did you go to bed?

Homework! *Write sentences for tomorrow!*

I will get up at _____, I will have a shower …

60. Adjectives (words to describe)

good	big	little	funny
not bad	huge	small	amusing
pleasant +	large	tiny	hilarious ++
great! ++	gigantic	miniature	comical
fantastic ++	enormous	not very big!	
amazing +++			
superb +++			
interesting	**intelligent**	**happy**	**sad**
not boring	clever	content	unhappy
fascinating	smart	glad	down
informative	bright	pleased	miserable
educational	brainy	cheerful	
	talented		
beautiful (person)	**beautiful (place)**	**nice (person)**	**nice (thing)**
pretty (f.)	pretty	kind	lovely
good-looking	attractive	lovely	pleasant
handsome (m.)	stunning	warm	fantastic ++
attractive	lovely	friendly	
		helpful	
good food	**bad**	**exciting**	**Character:**
tasty	terrible	thrilling	quiet
delicious	awful	gripping	shy
yummy!	nasty		outgoing
superb ++	not good!		friendly
			funny

Describe:

- a person
- a film
- a place
- how you are feeling today!

Comparing adjectives:

adjective	comparing	superlative
small	smaller than	the smallest
important	**more important than**	**the most important**
good	better than	the best
bad	worse than	the worst

Short adjectives: add **-er** to compare, **-est** for the superlative

Longer adjectives: **more + adjective** to compare, **the most + adjective** for the superlative.

Two syllable adjectives ending in -y follow the pattern for short adjectives (but change the 'y' to 'I' when you write) e.g. easy, lazy, tidy, pretty, tiny, lovely…

This is the easiest part of today's lesson.

My son is lazier than my daughter.

This is the prettiest village in England!

Compare two places…

then compare two or three films.

61. Distances

EDINBURGH									
290	BIRMINGHAM								
373	102	CARDIFF							
496	185	228	DOVER						
193	110	208	257	LEEDS					
214	90	165	270	73	LIVERPOOL				
412	118	150	81	191	198	LONDON			
222	86	173	285	41	34	201	MANCHESTER		
112	207	301	360	94	155	288	141	NEWCASTLE	
186	129	231	264	25	97	194	66	82	YORK

Miles or kilometres?

1 mile = 1.61 km

5 miles = 8 kilometres

Work with a partner: one of you asks "How far is it from _____ to _____?"

Talk about distances in a country you know e.g.

"The capital is about 50 miles from the coast. My town is about 120 miles from the capital."

Note: to make the comparative of 'far', we uses 'further':

I go shopping in Coventry. I sometimes go to Birmingham, but it is further away.

62. A famous town/comparisons

Stratford-upon-Avon

Stratford-upon Avon is a town in Warwickshire, 22 miles south-east of Birmingham. It is 91 miles north-west of London. The population is about thirty thousand. It is a beautiful small town on the banks of the River Avon, and it is always busy with tourists. This is mainly because it was the birthplace and home for many years of William Shakespeare, the most famous writer in the history of Britain. He lived from 1564 to 1616, and he wrote plays (such as *Romeo and Juliet* and *Hamlet*) which are famous all over the world. He also wrote poetry, and is generally regarded as a master of the English language. Today the town has a fine theatre, home to the Royal Shakespeare Company. There are many nice shops and cafés, and there are often market stalls. The town centre is always lively, and the quality of the street musicians is normally very good. You can take a boat on the river, but be careful – the water is not very warm if you fall in!

Complete the chart about Stratford, then talk about it using the chart:

County?	*Warwickshire*	Birthplace of...	
Distance to London		There are...	
population		You can...	

Write some notes about a town or a city you know, then talk about it using your notes. Your notes could include:

- Country

- Distance to the capital

- Population

- There is.../There are...

- You can...

Revision: Comparisons

You can compare two places like this:

Stratford is **bigger** than Dunchurch but **smaller** than Birmingham.

Short adjectives add -er

*My brother is **older** than me.*

*Use these tennis balls – they are **newer**.*

Longer adjectives use "more + adjective"

*Stratford is **more famous** than Dunchurch. In my opinion, Coventry is **more interesting** than Birmingham.*

Short adjectives ending -y change to -ier

*My room is **tidier** now!*

*This lesson is **easier**! Last week it was more difficult.*

'good' and 'bad'

'good' changes to 'better', and 'bad' changes to 'worse':

This hotel is better than the last one.

Was 'Top Gun 2' better or worse than 'Top Gun 1' in your opinion?

63. Directions: Welcome to Esoltown!

You arrive in Esoltown from the south, you leave the main road in the direction of the town centre, then stop your car to ask someone for help...

Visitor: Excuse me, can you tell me the way to the amazon warehouse?

Local person: Yes, certainly. Turn left, go straight on. Go to the traffic lights, continue straight on, then take the first street on the left after the traffic lights.

Visitor: So, straight on, straight on at the traffic lights and first left after the lights.

Local person: That's it. Go under a bridge and the amazon warehouse is on the left.

Visitor: So, under a bridge and it's on the left.

Local person: Yes. You can't miss it!

Visitor: Thank you very much. I'm a bit early for my appointment. Can I park in the town centre?

Local person: Yes, go straight on through the town centre until you come to a roundabout. Take the first exit and you will see a big car park.

Visitor: Thank you for your help

Local person: You're welcome!

Look at the map of Esoltown. What number is the amazon warehouse? Read the conversation with a partner, them change the roles and read it again.

Here are some common directions that you may hear from a local person or from your Satnav!

Turn left
Turn right
Take the first/second/third street on the left/right
Go straight on
At the traffic lights...
At the roundabout
It's the first/second/third building on the left/right

 Go to the crossroads... At the crossroads, turn left/turn right/go straight on...

 Go to the roundabout.... At the roundabout... Take the first/second/third exit

Go to the traffic lights... At the (traffic) lights...

Go under the bridge/Go over the bridge.

Practise the expressions with your teacher!

Sometimes we give directions by referring to a well-known place

Go past the library. It's on the right.

You will see the station on your left.

If you see the leisure centre, you have gone too far! Turn back!

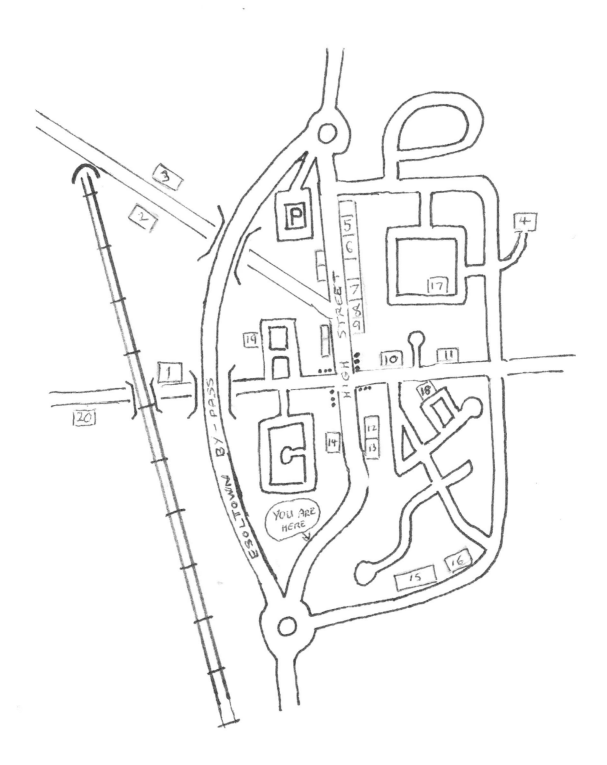

Some of the buildings on the map have numbers.

- What number is the station, do you think?

- Your teacher will give you directions to three other places: can you identify the numbers? Start each time from the point on the map marked "You are here".

In Esoltown there is...

- a station
- a leisure centre
- a primary school
- a doctor's surgery
- a library
- an art gallery

There are also...

- two banks
- shops, including a general store, a baker's and a butcher's
- several small companies

and a lot of residential streets (streets with houses and apartments).

-
- Work with a partner. One of you asks the way to a place, the other finds it on the map.
- Change the roles!
- One of you can give directions to a house somewhere in the residential streets, the other listens carefully and puts a finger on the map to show you have understood.

64. Conversation: I need to see a doctor

(You will need to practise parts of the body)

Receptionist: Good morning, Doctor's surgery, can I help you?

Patient: Good morning. I need to see a doctor

Receptionist: Can you describe the problem, please?

Patient: My (ankle) hurts and I can't (walk)

Receptionist: I see. How long have you had the problem?

Patient: For (two) days.

Receptionist: How did it start?

Patient: I played football/ I don't know.

Receptionist: Can I have your name, please?

Patient: _____ _____

Receptionist: Can you spell that, please?

Patient: _ _ _ _   _ _ _ _ _ _ _ _

Receptionist: And your date of birth?

Patient: It's the __ of (November) 19_ _

Receptionist: Is the address (*your address*)?

Patient: Yes, that's right.

Receptionist: Can you come (Friday) at (10.30)

Patient: Yes, that's fine. See you on (Friday) at (10.30).Thank you!

Receptionist: You're welcome. Goodbye.

65. Talking about your life (2)

Can you say some simple sentences about your life so far?

I was born in _____ (year?)

I grew up in _____ (place)

I went to school in _____ (place) for _____ years

I left (country) in _____ (because?)

I moved to England in _____ (year?)

If you have worked...	If you are a young person...
I left school at the age of___	I started school at the age of _____
I trained as a(n) _____	I went to (*name or type of school*) in
I got a job in _____	_____ for ____ years.
I stayed there for ___ years/months	I left that school at the age of _____.
I was unemployed for ___ years/months	I came to England.

Questions about a person's life – choose the missing word from the box:

When _____ you born?	Date of birth?
Where _____ you born?	Birthplace?
When _____ you start school?	Age you started school?
How long _____ you stay at this school?	How long?
When ___ you leave school?	Age you left school?
What did you ___ then?	Then?
How long _____ you unemployed?	Unemployed how long?
What _____ your first job?	First job?
Why did _____ leave your country?	Reason for leaving?
When ___ you arrive in the UK?	Arrival in the UK?

do	did	was	were	you

Now work in pairs to ask a person about their life.

66. Sports and hobbies

I like	playing	football.
		chess.
		tennis.
		frisbee.
I don't like	watching	rugby.
		pool.
		computer games.
		cricket.
	walking.	
	cooking.	
	sewing.	
	drawing.	
	painting.	

Cricket

Choose one of the words as you listen to the presentation (script at the end of the unit*) about the popular English sport of Cricket.

1. There are **[two/three/four]** teams – one team 'bats' (tries to hit the ball to score), the other team 'fields' (tries to stop the batting team from scoring by standing around the field and stopping or catching the ball).

2. Each team has **[nine/ten/eleven]** players, but when the team is batting, only two players are on the field at a time.

3. The batting players try to hit the ball and run before the fielders can stop them reaching the other end of the central strip (called the 'wicket'), so the score in cricket is measured in 'runs'. If the batter hits the ball past the edge of the field ('the boundary'), he/she scores **[three/four/five]** runs, and if he hits it over the edge without touching the ground, it is six runs!

4. But if the bowler (the member of the fielding team who throws the ball) hits one of the **[two/three/four]** pieces of wood behind the batter ('the stumps'), he/she is 'out', and the next member of the team replaces him/her. The batter can also be out if he/she hits the ball to a fielder and the fielder catches it before it touches the ground. A third reason that a

player can be out is if the fielder hits the stumps before the batter reaches the other end of the wicket.

5. When [**nine/ten/eleven**] of the eleven batters are out, the score they have reached is the target for the other team. The two teams exchange their roles and the other team tries to score more.

6. There are variations, particularly limiting the time that each team has (otherwise games can last a very long time!). The game is played in units of six called 'an over', after which they change ends and a different bowler must be used. Many matches have [**ten/twenty/thirty**] overs for each team, meaning that the match lasts for about three hours.

 a batter (or batsman/batswoman)

Try to simply describe your favourite sport to another person.

It is a team sport. There are _____ players in each team.

(OR: It is an individual sport.)

The equipment you need is_____. It is (not) expensive.

You play on a special place called _____ (a pitch/a court/ a course...).

You score points by _____ (getting the ball in a goal/hitting the ball past your opponent/ hitting a target...).

A game lasts _____ minutes/hours/days.

It is good for _____ (fitness/meeting people...).

*Script for presentation

Cricket is a team game, but the **two** teams are not all on the field at the same time: one team 'bats' (tries to hit the ball to score), the other team 'fields' (tries to stop the batting team from scoring by standing around the field and stopping or catching the ball). It can be a bit complicated! The best way to learn the game is to watch a game. Each team has **eleven** players, but when the team is batting, only two players are on the field at a time. The batting players try to hit the ball and run before the fielders can stop them reaching the other end of the central strip (called the 'wicket'), so the score in cricket is measured in 'runs'. If the batter hits the ball past the edge of the field ('the boundary'), he/she scores **four** runs, and if he hits it over the edge without touching the ground, it is six runs! However, the eleven players fielding can eliminate the batter in several ways. If the bowler (the member of the fielding team who throws the ball) hits one of the **three** pieces of wood behind the batter ('the stumps'), he/she is 'out', and the next member of the team replaces him/her. The batter can also be out if he/she hits the ball to a fielder and the fielder catches it before it touches the ground. A third reason that a player can be out is if, while the batters are running, the fielder hits the stumps before the batter reaches the other end of the wicket. When **ten** of the eleven batters are out, the score they have reached is the target for the other team. The two teams exchange their roles and the other team tries to score more. There are variations, particularly limiting the time that each team has (otherwise games can last a very long time!). The game is played in units of six called 'an over', after which they change ends and a different bowler must be used. Many matches have **twenty** overs for each team, meaning that the match lasts for about three hours. A new version that you may see on television is called "The Hundred", where the bowling team bowls the ball a hundred times. A full international match can last five days!

67. Revision: the simple past tense

The simple past tense is actually the most frequent verb tense, so it's important to get it right.

- In positive verbs, you use one word (ending in '-ed' for regular verbs.)
- For negatives and questions, use 'did' + verb

Positive:

I/you/he/she/it/we/they	played
	worked
	watched
	had
	went
	ate
	drank
I/ he/she/it	was
You/we/they	were

Negative:

I/you/he/she/it/we/they	did not do (much)
	did not go
	did not eat
But: I/he/she/it	was not
You/we/they	were not

Questions:

Did you do anything interesting?

Where did you go?

What did you have to eat?

Were you tired?

Was the weather nice?

A survey: ask five people about their weekend!

Name	Main activity?	Where?	Ate?	Watched?	other

Here are some questions: use them for the first two people, then try to remember them as you repeat with persons 3, 4 and 5.

Main activity: What did you do at the weekend?

Where? Where did you go?

Ate? What did you (have to) eat?

Watched? Did you watch anything?

Other information: (you could use any of these questions or your own question)

Was it a good weekend? What was the weather like? Were you very tired? Did you enjoy the film? Did you enjoy the meal? Who did you go with?

68. At the bank

A person arriving from abroad goes to the bank to open an account. Listen as your teacher and a helper read the conversation and note the name that he/she gives. The read the conversation with a partner.

Bank employee: Good morning. How can I help you?

Customer: Good morning. I would like to open an account, please.

BE: Certainly. What sort of account?

C: I need an account with a payment card.

BE: You'll need to speak to one of our advisers. Can I take your name, please?

C: Yes, it's _____ _____.

BE: Can you spell that, please?

C: _ _ _ _ _   _ _ _ _ _ ...

BE: Thank you. Do you have proof of identity and proof of address?

C: I have a passport. What do I need for proof of address?

BE: Something like an electricity bill, or a Council Tax bill.

C: I'm afraid I don't have those as I am staying in a hotel/I am staying with a host family.

BE: I see. You can discuss this with our adviser. Please take a seat.

C: Thank you.

69. Jobs

Practise saying these words for jobs: you may need to use a dictionary to check the meanings.

a student   a teacher   an engineer   a doctor   a nurse

a plumber   an electrician   a mechanic   a pharmacist

an office worker   a waiter/a waitress   a cook/a chef

a care assistant   a technician   a dentist   a computer programmer

a businessman/businesswoman   a hairdresser   a gardener

Some other useful words:

retired   unemployed   a housewife/a house husband

What would you like to do in the future?

Talk about people you know:

Present tense*:*

My brother is a(n) _____.

My friend, (John), is a(n) _____.

My sister... My son ...

Past tense:

Before I was ...

(You could say "My occupation was teacher/plumber/electrician etc.").

My parents were ...

Your career history

Look back at the units on "Talking about your life". Write about your career history (the details of jobs you had). Include some important details from your education. When you are ready, read your sentences to a partner.

Here is an example:

I went to school at the age of six and when I was sixteen, I took the school-leaving examinations. My best subject was maths, but I also enjoyed arts subjects such as music and art. I went to college for two years and studied art and design. At the age of eighteen I worked in an architect's office for two years. The job was not very interesting, so I left and I looked for a job in fashion. It was difficult to find anything, so for eight months I worked in a clothes shop. Then I got a job in the office of a clothes factory. It was more interesting, but I did not stay in the job because of the war in my country. I came to England a year ago.

Remember: negative verbs in the past use "did" + verb except "was/were"

It was not very interesting.

The people were not very friendly.

I did not like the job.

I did not stay there because...

I did not go to university.

"didn't" or "did not"?

When you speak, it is normal to use the shorter "didn't", but when you write, use the full version "did not"

70. The application form

Can you fill in this form in BLOCK LETTERS (Capital letters)?

Title													
First name													
Surname													
DOB													
Postcode													
House no.													
Nationality													
Telephone													

Possible answers for 'Title'

MR for a man

MS for a woman

MRS if a woman prefers to identify as married

MISS if a woman prefers to identify as not married

DOB = Date of birth: If you have six boxes (as here), fill in day/month/year

So if you have a birthday on 7th October and were born in 2002, you fill in:

0	7	1	0	0	2

Male [ ]   Female [ ]

Marital status:

Single [ ]   Married [ ]   Widowed [ ]   Separated [ ]   Divorced [ ]

Maiden Name: This is a woman's surname before marriage

Spouse: This can be husband or wife

Occupation: asks about a job if you have one

On the phone:

Now imagine that you are giving the information over the phone (for example, to buy an insurance policy). Practise answering the questions with a friend. You can always invent details that you don't want to say!

Can I have your surname please?

Can you spell that please?

And your first name?

Can you spell that for me, please?

Your marital status?

(What was your maiden name, please?)

What's your date of birth?

And a postcode, please?

What's the house number or name?

And your telephone number please?

What was your most recent occupation?

And finally your nationality?

71. Manners

Some small phrases will help you to make a better impression when you meet people.

1. 'Please' and 'Thank you': use them as much as you can!
   Can you help me, please?
   Could I have a drink, please?
   (when someone offers you something) Y*es, please/No thank you.*
   (when you receive something or someone has helped you) *Thank you very much*

2. 'May', 'would' and 'could' are used in polite situations:
   'may' is used for permission: *May I come in? May I sit here? May I go now?*
   'Would you like…' is the same as 'Do you want…' but is more polite:
   'Would you like a cup of coffee? Would you like me to help?'
   Sometimes you can replace 'can' with 'could' to be more polite: *Could I have some more pizza, please? 'Could you help me, please?'*
   (notice that we still say 'please'!)

3. Some good phrases:
   I'm sorry to bother you: *could you help me please?*
   If it's not too much trouble (when you want help with something, or someone offers to help you)
   Thank you, that's kind of you (when someone offers you help, for example, to give you a lift somewhere in their car)
   That would be lovely! (you are very happy to be offered something)

   Look at these examples:
   A friendly person: *I have some children's toys that we don't need, would you like me to bring them for your children?*
   You: *That would be lovely! Thank you very much.*

   You: *I'm sorry to bother you. Could you help me please? I can't open this door.*

   You: *Could I have some more vegetables, please?*
   Chef: *Certainly, here you are.*
   You: *Thank you, that's kind of you.*

4. 'Excuse me': When you start to speak, especially if you interrupt people who are talking to each other, it's a good idea to start with 'Excuse me':
   - Excuse me, please, is this the correct room for the English lesson?
   - Excuse me, could you help me, please? I need to see a doctor.

You have an appointment with a lawyer: choose one of the phrases from the box under the conversation to complete it.

You: _____1._____ I have an appointment with Mr Robson.

Receptionist: Can I have your name, please?

You: It's …. …….

Receptionist: I'll tell him you're here. Please take a seat.

You: _____2._____, could I have a glass of water, please?

Receptionist: Certainly, I'll get you one.

You: Thank you, _____3._____.

Receptionist: Would you like a cup of tea or coffee?

You: _____4._____. Coffee, please.

Receptionist: Milk and sugar?

You: No,_____5._____, just a black coffee.

Receptionist: I'll bring it to you in Mr Robson's office. Come this way, please.

If it's not too much trouble…….thank you………That's very kind of you……..

That would be lovely…….May I come in? ………Excuse me, could you help me?

Now practise reading the conversation with a partner.

72. More on modal verbs (can, will, must…)

Fill in the blanks:

I _____ speak a little English, but I _____ to learn more. Next week I _____ attend the English class. I _____ do some homework before the class. I _____ be late as the class starts at 10.00 o'clock, and I _____ do some washing before that.

may	must	can	will	would like

"I may be late" can mean "There is a possibility I will be late"

'will' and **'shall'** are both used to talk about the future. There are fine differences, but 'will' is much more frequently used.

Remember: to make questions and negatives, you do not need "do/does" with modal verbs e.g.

Shall I take your coat? Can you help me? You mustn't be late!

You cannot (= can not) be serious!

Alternatives:

must	have to
can	am/is/are able to
may	am/is/are allowed to
may (possibility)	there is a possibility I/you… will

Examples:

I must go now = I have to go now.

We may go into town = We are allowed to go into town.

Can you come earlier? = Are you able to come earlier?

You may find the traffic is bad on a Friday = There is a possibility you will find the traffic is bad on a Friday.

Two reasons why the alternatives are important:

1. You cannot use two modal verbs together (e.g. ~~will can~~), so use the alternative e.g. "After six months you will be allowed to attend college"

2. Past tenses: The safest way to make a past tense of the modal verb is to use the alternative form:

   Last week I had to stay in my room because I was ill. I was not able to attend the English class. I was not allowed to leave the hotel.

Practise by putting these sentences into the past:

I must go into to town   → Yesterday I .....

I cannot understand this document   → I .....

I may not leave until six o'clock   → I ...

And now make these sentences future:

I can see you   → Next week I .....

You must get up early   → Tomorrow you ...

Look at the table on the next page and the alternative phrases below the table: which is the correct match for each of the modal verbs?

Write the correct phrase next to each verb, or if you don't want to write on the book, copy the table into your exercise book or on paper.

can -	
could -	
will -	
would + verb -	
would like to -	
may (1) -	
may (2)	
must -	

- To have to, expresses an obligation
- Similar to 'want' but more polite
- To talk about the future
- To be allowed to, expresses permission
- To be able to, have the ability (often "Is it OK to...?")
- Used in place of 'can' to be more polite, conditional (and past) form of 'can'
- Expresses a possibility, but is not certain
- Conditional form of 'will'

'might' is similar to 'may' in the sense of an uncertain possibility:

It might rain tomorrow.

I might be late.

(There are some other modal verbs -we will learn about 'shall', 'should' and 'ought to' later!)

73. Experiences: the present perfect tense

In English, we use **"have" + past participle***...

- for something which started in the past and continues:
  I have lived in Rugby for one year. I have been at the hotel for three months.
- for experiences which may be repeated in the future:
  Have you been to London? No, I have never been there, but I would like to go there in the future.
  I have taken an aeroplane three times.

  *The past participle is the same as the past tense for regular verbs: ending -ed
  For irregular verbs, some are the same as the past tense (e.g. *had, got, slept, bought*...) but for others you need to learn the past participle spelling.
  Here are a few:

verb	Past tense	Past participle
be (is, am, are)	was, were	been
see	saw	seen
take	took	taken
sing	sang	sung
eat	ate	eaten
go	went	gone

Some questions (and possible answers)

Have you been in England long?	Not very long – I've been here about five months.
Have you been to the doctor?	No, I haven't.
Have you had a Covid vaccination?	Yes – I have had two vaccinations.
Have you visited Coventry?	No, not yet. I haven't had the opportunity.
What jobs have you done?	I have worked as a _____
Have you ever eaten snails?	Yes, three times, I think.
Have you had any criminal convictions?	No, I haven't!

129

74. A job interview

(This conversation uses the past tense and the present perfect tense)

This is a conversation you might have if you apply for a job, for example a voluntary job helping in a charity shop.

Practise reading this conversation with a partner, then change some of it so that the information is correct for yourself!

Manager: Good afternoon. I'm John Smith/ Jane Smith, the manager.

Person applying for a post: Good afternoon, I'm _____. Pleased to meet you.

Thank you for coming. Did it take you long to get here?

No, only half an hour.

Can you tell me a bit about yourself?

Certainly. I come from _____. I'm ____ years old.

How long have you been in England?

I've been in England for _____ years/months, and I have lived here for ____ months.

I see. And what jobs have you done?

In _____ I trained as a _____ / I worked as a _____

Have you ever worked in a (shop)?

No, I haven't / Yes, I worked in a _____ (shop) in _____.

Why did you leave your country (if you don't mind my asking)?

There was a war and it was very dangerous /I prefer not to talk about it

And why would you like to work/volunteer here?

I think your organisation is very good and I would like to help.

What kind of a person would you say you are?

I'm sorry. I don't quite understand the question...

Can you describe your character? Are you outgoing? Shy? Honest?

I see. I think I am quite outgoing. I like meeting people, and yes, I am honest and trustworthy.

What times and days are you available?

Any time that suits you!

Perhaps you could come next Monday for a trial?

Take note: "have got" is used as an alternative to "have" in the present simple: *Have you got a pen? I haven't got any cash, have you?*

At the end of an interview, people often ask:
"Have you got any questions?"

75. Pronunciation (stress)

Spoken English has strong syllables* and weak syllables, so it is important both for understanding and to pronounce well.

A syllable* is the beat, for example the word "United" has three syllables. The strong syllable is the second – Unİted. We also call this the 'stressed syllable'.

Stress in words

Words with more than one syllable are likely to have a strong syllable, with the others reduced to a minimum.

For example, the country Canada has the stress on the first syllable, and the other two syllables are minimum sounds – Can 'd '

How do we know which is the strong syllable? There are a few patterns…

1. The syllable before -tion: nation, national, international, internationalist. *Try saying these words: communication, production, perfectionist*

2. Most syllables before -ic: electric, electrical, basic. *Try saying these words: electronic, fantastic, political.* (Exceptions include electricity, politician, politics)

3. Most syllables before -ity: electricity, brevity, community. *Try saying these words: calamity, gravity, reciprocity*

4. Stress the syllable before with countries and regions ending -ia: Bulgaria, Nigeria, Romania. *Try saying these countries and regions: Bavaria, Slovenia, Namibia.* (Tanzania is an exception)

Stress in the sentence

The stressed syllables in the sentence are normally the most important words, the ones which add new information. So words like "is", "was", modal verbs are not normally stressed (though negatives are stressed). Some examples:

You can visit the house on Tuesday. You can't come tomorrow – there won't be anyone here.

Imagine a helper at your class is collecting pens at the end of the lesson:

Helper: Can I have your p**e**n please?

Student: I gave it to the t**ea**cher

The important word in the question is "pen" and the important word in the answer is "teacher". The other words are not very important – the conversation could simply be:

Helper: Pen?

Student: Teacher!

Probably both of them would understand, even just with the one word!

It's difficult to make rules about which words to stress. Listen to people speaking, and try to observe how they stress words. None of the suggestions below is 100% sure – we can vary the stress if we want to emphasise. For example, prepositions are often not stressed, but if it is the most important word, we stress it!

- *Did you say my laptop was on the desk?*
- *No, I said it was **U**nder the desk.*

Not often stressed	Often stressed
The verb 'to be' (*am/is/are/was/were*) Modal verbs (*can, could, will, would, must...*) Articles (*the/a/an*) Prepositions	Nouns (especially the first time they are mentioned) Adjectives (they usually give new information) Verbs (especially if the verb gives key information)

Try reading this text. Mark some of the stress before you start reading.

My home town is in Essex. There is a famous market, but it is not very beautiful. You can get to London easily, so if you like theatres or museums, you will find them nearby. The population is about thirty thousand, and many people work in London. The community is very international, with a high proportion of people of Asian origin, and a significant number from Poland, Romania and Bulgaria.

76. More on countable and uncountable nouns

Revise Unit 40 about Countable and Uncountable Nouns.

Look at the short text at the end of Unit 74 on Pronunciation (stress) starting "My home town is in Essex": are these words countable or uncountable?

theatres

market

town

people

The answer? They are all countable, "theatres" and "people" are plurals, and we could make plurals of "town" and "market" by adding -s.

Take a piece of paper and write the headings 'countable' or 'uncountable' at the top of two columns...

Countable	Uncountable

Read the text below. The nouns are underlined – put them in the countable or uncountable column.

It can be difficult to find <u>accommodation</u> in Britain. You find <u>flats</u> and <u>houses</u> for <u>rent</u> with <u>an estate agent</u>, but you need to pay <u>a fee</u> to <u>the estate agent</u> and pay <u>the rent</u> in advance, so it can be expensive. Then you have to find <u>furniture.</u> You can buy some <u>things</u> quite cheaply in <u>charity shops</u>. If you don't have much <u>money,</u> the local council may offer some <u>help</u>. Do you have any <u>questions</u>?

Reminder: types of uncountable nouns:

- concepts e.g. **money, cash, happiness, information, knowledge, travel, work**

- group nouns e.g. **furniture, accommodation, baggage, traffic**

- substances e.g. many food words – **food, rice, pasta, cheese*, meat**

- school subjects e.g**. history, maths, English, art, music...**

Here are a few more words for you to consider: countable or uncountable?

roundabout, education, economics, road, burger, television, basketball, circle, elephant, car, history, engineering, factory, office, meat.

True or False?

1. You can't use 'a' (or 'an') with an uncountable noun.
2. In this question, we can put an uncountable noun in the space: "How many _____ do you have?"
3. In this statement, we can put an uncountable noun in the space: "I have got a lot of _____ in my garden."
4. The word "much" cannot be before a countable noun.

Read this conversation with a partner: when there is a choice, can you decide which word fits best?

Person A: I'd like (1) fish/carrot for my lunch. I hope there are (2) chips/meat with it.

Person B: That sounds good. I think I will have (3) bean/rice.

A: Does your daughter go to a (4) school/history?

B: Yes. She has many (5) friend/friends.

A: That's good. What is her favourite (6) subject/subjects?

B: She likes (7) garden/music. She would like to have a (8) guitar/education for her music lessons.

A: How much is the (9) instrument/instruments she wants?

B: Too much (10) money/pounds! Maybe we can find her a second-hand instrument.

77. Questions and answers

Often the verb in the question can be used in the answer:

What **is** your name?	My name **is** _____ _____
Where do you **come from**?	I **come from** _____
How long **have** you **been** in England?	I **have been** here for ___ months/years.
What **would** you **like** to do in the future?	I **would like** to become a(n) _____.
Where **are** you **going** after this?	I **am going** to _____.

This doesn't always work, especially where the verb in the question is "do":

What are you doing?	I am filling in a form.
What did you do before?	I was (a taxi driver/unemployed).
What do you do in the afternoons?	Sometimes I play football with friends, sometimes I stay in my room.
Can I have your name, please?	Certainly, it's _____ _____
How do you get to Coventry?	I take the bus.

Practise these questions with a partner.

Question words:

Where ? – the answer is a place

When? – the answer is a time

How long? – the answer is a length of time

Why? – the answer is a reason, often using "because"

How? – the answer is a method

How far? – the answer is a distance

Which ___? – the answer is one of a choice of two or three options

Who? – the answer is a person

How much/How many? – the answer is a price or a quantity

Match up these questions to the answer !

When did you get up this morning?	*In the Town Hall*
How long did it take to get to Coventry?	*Because I had an appointment*
How far is it?	*Number 72*
Why did you go into Coventry?	*At seven o'clock*
Where was your appointment?	*About forty minutes*
Which bus did you take?	*About fifteen kilometres*

Now try to answer these questions:

What do you do in the evenings?	
What did you do yesterday evening?	
How long have you been in (Rugby)?	
Where would you like to live in the future? Why?	
How long does it take to walk to the town centre?	
Have you ever been into Coventry?	
When did go there?	
How did you get to Coventry?	

Longer answers:

Conversations are not normally like this! In most conversations, one person tells the other one about something using several sentences. Read the examples, then answer the questions below with a long answer.

What did you do at the weekend?	*Not very much. I got up late on Saturday, so I didn't get any breakfast. I stayed in my room in the morning, then after lunch I played football with some friends. We watched a film in the evening. On Sunday I went for a walk and played computer games. That's all*
Can you tell me about your journey here?	*It was quite difficult. When I arrived in England, I had to stay in a centre for a few weeks while my application was processed. Then I was taken by bus to a hotel. I think it took about two hours. I didn't stay there long – maybe four days, then I was transferred here. I came by bus, and it took about four hours. It wasn't very comfortable.*

What do you do in your free time?

Can you tell me about your life?

Describe a friend or family member.

Tell me about the film you watched.

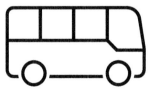

78. Conversation: Problems on the phone:

Hello.	Hello. Can I speak to Mr Carter, please?
Who's calling?	My name is _____ _____
I'm sorry, can you spell that, please?	Yes. _ _ _ _ _ _ then _ _ _ _ _ _
Thank you. hold the line please…	
I'm sorry, he's on another call at the moment	I see. Could you ask him to call me back?
Yes, what's the number?	It's _ _ _ _ _ _ _ _ _ _ _
Thank you. I'll give him the message.	Thank you very much, goodbye

Do the conversation again, but the receptionist can change the bold sentence
(**I'm sorry, he's on another call at the moment**) and use another sentence
"He's away this week" – can you respond in the right way?

79. London

London is the capital city of England and of the United Kingdom. The Houses of Parliament are in Westminster, which is in the west of the city. Its famous clock tower contains the bell of Big Ben. In the east there is the business district, often called 'The City'. The Tower of London is also in the east: it is a castle and was sometimes used as a prison, but today it is a museum that you can visit. A lot of other attractions are in the west of the city near the parliament – for example, there is the National Gallery, one of the most famous art galleries in the world. It is on Trafalgar Square, which has a famous column in the middle with a statue of Nelson, a nineteenth century admiral. There are also a lot of statues near the parliament – most of them of British people but there are also statues of Mahatma Gandhi and Nelson Mandela. About a mile from the Houses of Parliament is Buckingham Palace, which is the London residence of the monarch.

The population is about 8 million, but most of these people do not live in the centre. It is very expensive to live in the centre of London, so a lot of people commute by train or bus. The train from Rugby to London takes less than an hour, so there are even commuters who live here. It is not easy to drive in the centre of London – it's better to take a red bus, or use the Underground trains.

Reminder: Comparing things

London is bigger than Birmingham. It is more important and is better for transport networks.

*We add **-er** to short adjectives, but with longer adjectives we use '**more +***

Superlatives

In fact, London is not only bigger than Birmingham – it is bigger than all other English towns and cities: **it is the biggest!**

It is also **the most important** city. It is the financial and political centre of the UK. With its Underground railway and network of buses, it has **the best** transport system in the UK.

Superlatives are formed like this:

- **'the adjective + -est'** for short adjectives (e.g. the shortest, the longest)
- **'the most + adjective'** for longer adjectives (e.g. the most interesting)
- good → **'the best'** and bad → **'the worst'**

Using the adjective in brackets, complete this text about the city of Rome.

Rome is [amazing] _____place I know. It has some of [old]_____

buildings in the world. It is [big]_____ city in Italy, and as the parliament is

there we can say it is [important]_____. It has some of [good]

_____pizza restaurants, but unfortunately some of [bad] _____traffic

in Europe!

-

What about places in your country? What is the nicest place? And the most important? Where is the best restaurant? Where is the most spectacular view? And the highest mountain? What is the longest river?

Talk to a partner about your country using some superlative adjectives!

80. Conversation at the school gates

Look at the conversation between two parents waiting for their children outside the school gates and read it with a partner. (One part of the conversation is on the next page)

(The first person)

- Hello, you're Sophie's mum/ dad, aren't you?

- I'm Olivia's mum/dad. They are good friends.

- *Where do you come from?

- *How many children do you have?

- I have two: Olivia has an older brother.

- *How long have you been in England?

- *Do you like it here?

- It's cold in winter. What is the winter like in your country?

- Perhaps Sophie could come to our house to play with Olivia one day after school?

- What about next Monday?

- I can't do Tuesday, what about Wednesday?

- I'll give them some tea and you can pick Sophie up at about 6.30?

- I'll write down all the details, and my phone number…

- Is there anything Sophie doesn't eat?

- That's fine. Oh, here they come – they'll be pleased!

(The second person)

- Yes. Who is your child?

- Oh yes, Sophie often talks about Olivia.

- I come from Brazil.

- Just one/two/three...and you?

- That's nice, you have a boy and a girl.

- Six months

- Yes, people are friendly. But it's a bit cold!

- It's warmer than here.

- That sounds nice, thank you.

- Oh, I'm sorry, next Monday is not convenient.

- Yes, Wednesday is fine. How long for?

- OK, can you tell me the address, please?

- Thank you so much!

- She doesn't like fish, but she'll eat most things.

- Yes! Sophie will be very pleased. Thank you again.

*Read the conversation again, changing some of the details. If you are the first person, change the order of you questions with * so that the second person has to listen carefully and respond correctly!*

81. Birmingham – England's second city

Birmingham is England's second-largest city (after London). It is difficult to be precise about its population, as there are a large number of people who live in the surrounding towns and villages of the West Midlands region. About 2 million people live in the city of Birmingham, but the Birmingham area has about 4 million.

There is a cathedral, and there are many churches, mosques, temples and other places of worship in the city, which has a diverse, multi-ethnic population. It is an important cultural centre, with plenty of cinemas, concert halls, theatres, sporting venues and museums. The City of Birmingham Symphony Orchestra is famous all over the world. There are 5 universities, including the well-established University of Birmingham just south of the city centre.

It is about 100 miles north-west of London. It is perhaps unusual that there is not a major river running through Birmingham, but it has more canals than Venice, so you are never far from water! Its position in the centre of the country has aided the development of industry and commerce. Manufacturing is not as important as it was in the past, but there is a vibrant service sector.

It has an airport south-east of the city, near a large exhibition complex, the NEC (the National Exhibition Centre). There are many shops, entertainment venues, sporting facilities… it is hard to think of something that Birmingham doesn't have!

Understanding the text

Are these sentences true or false?

1. People from many different cultures live in the Birmingham area.
2. There is a large river running through the centre of the city.
3. A lot of people work in manufacturing.
4. London is to the south-east of Birmingham.
5. You can see major sporting events in the city.
6. It is a good place to hear top-quality classical music.

Describing a place

			comments
It is	100 miles north-west	of London	*(distance from capital or another well-known place)*
There is		a cathedral, an airport	*(only one)*
There are	(a lot of, many, plenty of)	shops, places of worship, entertainment venues, sporting venues	*(plural)*
It has		an airport, five universities	*(singular or plural)*
It doesn't have	any	a major river mountains	*(any + plural)*

Use the table to describe a place you know.

"its" or "it's"?

"It's" is short for "it is". If there is no apostrophe, it is the possessive adjective (belonging to 'it') – as in the text above "It is difficult to be precise about **its** population"

82. At the doctor's

Do you know all these parts of the body?

head	eye(s)	ear(s)	nose	mouth
neck/throat	back			
arm	elbow	wrist	hand	finger(s)
chest	stomach			
leg	hip	knee		
ankle	foot/feet	toe(s)		

Practise describing problems to a doctor

I have hurt my...	back/arm/leg/knee...
I have a pain in my ...	wrist/ankle/hip/foot...
I have a (n)	headache/stomach ache/earache
I have a sore...	throat

Answering the doctor's questions:

Normally you need the same verb tense in the question and the answer:

- **Present tense:** *Where does it hurt? - It hurts here !*

- **Present Perfect Tense:** *How long have you had the pain? – I've had it for 2 days.*

- **Past tense:** *When did it start? – it started on Tuesday.*

Practise by answering these questions:

When did it happen? How many times have you taken paracetamol today? Are you allergic to penicillin? What did you have for breakfast?

Now work with a partner and read the conversation on the next page:

At the doctor's

Good afternoon. I'm doctor _____. How can I help today?

I have a pain in my chest

I see. Where does it hurt exactly?

Here [point to your chest!]

How long have you had the pain?

For two days

Did you do anything that caused the pain to start?

I worked in the garden in the morning, then the pain started in the afternoon.

I see. Was the gardening very strenuous?

Not really.

Have you taken paracetamol or another painkiller?

Yes. I have taken the maximum each day.

Have you eaten anything unusual?

No, I haven't.

I'm going to prescribe you a treatment. Take this to your chemist. If the pain continues, contact the surgery again.

Thank you. Goodbye.

Change roles and read the conversation again.

Change some of the details to describe a different problem (e.g. a sports injury) and read the conversation again. If you are the doctor, change your questions to fit the problem.

83. Short answers to questions

We often answer questions repeating the first part of the verb:

Have you got a fridge in your room? - Yes I have/No I haven't.

Do you have a fridge in your room? - Yes I do/No I don't.

Can you come to the party on Saturday? - Yes I can/No I can't

So in a question with 'do/does/did', the answer often finishes with 'do/does/did' (or 'don't/doesn't/didn't'):

Does your son speak English? – Yes, he does/No, he doesn't.

Did you watch the football yesterday? – Yes I did/No, I didn't

In a verb tense with two words, the first word often finishes the answer:

Present Perfect: Have you lived in Rugby for many years? Yes, I have/ No, I haven't.

Present Continuous: Are you going to the party on Saturday? – Yes, I am/No I'm not.

Modals: Will you go to college in September? – Yes, I will/ No, I won't (= will not)

But if is appropriate to say 'Please' or 'Thank you', it is better to use those, not the short answers. For example, if someone offers you something:

Would you like a cup of coffee? – Yes, please/No, thank you *(better than 'Yes, I would/No I wouldn't')*

I'm going into town. Do you want a lift? – Yes, please/No, thank you

Try to answer these questions:

1. May I come in? – Yes….

2. Do you watch television in the evening? -No …

3. Would you like a drink? – Yes….

4. Does your brother live in England? – No …

5. Are you watching the football at the moment? – No…

Checking if something is correct

This is similar to the short answers to questions. We sometimes say something and check whether it is right with a short tag on the end of our statement.

> Your daughter likes school, doesn't she?
>
> You go to boxing lessons, don't you?
>
> Hello. Nice to see you again. It's Marina, isn't it? (*checking the person's name*)
>
> You live in Bilton, don't you?
>
> You haven't been here very long, have you?
>
> You can't come to the party, can you?

Notice that if the sentence is positive, the tag is negative, and if the sentence is negative, the tag is positive!

Sometimes this is just asking if the other person agrees (e.g. when we are talking about the weather):

> It's a nice day, isn't it? – Yes, it is!
>
> It's raining outside, isn't it? – No, it isn't.

Try and complete this conversation:

Person 1: Hello. It's Yousuf, __ __?

Person 2: Yes, __ ___. Nice to see you again. It's not a very nice day, __ ___?

P1: No, ___ __ ___.Can you come to the party on Saturday?

P2: No, I ____. Are you going?

P1: Yes, I ___.

P2: I have to go to Birmingham.

P1: I see. Do you have family there?

P2: Yes, I ___.

P1: You've been here for six months now, ___ ____?

P2: Yes, I ____.

P1: Do you like it here?

P2: Yes, I ___. People are very friendly.

P1: That's good. Would you like to go for a coffee?

P2: No, __ ____. I have an appointment in 5 minutes.

P1: Well, nice to see you again, take care!

P2: Thank you, you too!

Check your answers, then read the conversation with a partner.

149

84. Cooking instructions

Do you know a lot of words for food and drink? Check any words from these cooking instructions in a dictionary if necessary.

Stuffed Peppers and Potato Bake

1. Prepare the vegetables: potatoes in 2cm cubes, onions in half rings, leeks in rings, squash in 2 cm cubes.
2. Toss potato and squash cubes in a little oil, and sprinkle with salt and pepper to taste. Lightly sprinkle with mixed herbs.
3. Heat oven to 190°C / 170°C Fan / Gas 5. Roast the potatoes and squash for 25 mins (covered with foil). Turn the potatoes, check they are softening. Add the onions and leeks and roast for a further 12-15 mins.
4. Meanwhile, halve the red peppers, scoop out the seeds etc and roast for 15-20 mins.
5. Chop and fry the mushrooms in a little oil, add a small tin of tomatoes (for moisture) and tinned mixed beans, and a sprinkle of mixed herbs.
6. Once the peppers are roasted, fill with the mushroom and bean mixture. Sprinkle some cherry tomatoes onto the potato bake, place the stuffed peppers on top, and return to the over for 10 mins. (Cheese can be sprinkled on top of the peppers for the final 10 mins if required).

Now talk about how to prepare one of your favourite dishes: here are some verbs you might need...

... chop

... fry

... roast

... boil

... halve

... fill

... sprinkle

... add

... toss

Or you can talk about where you put the ingredients...

... place in the oven

... cook in a saucepan

Grammar: Imperative verbs

In the recipe, we give instructions. This is easy – we just use the verb.

Chop and fry the mushrooms in a little oil, add a small tin of tomatoes...

To give a negative instruction, use "don't" + verb

Don't put in the flour until you have mixed the butter, sugar and eggs.

Don't use tinned tomatoes – fresh tomatoes taste better!

It's the same if you give an order, but adding "please" at the end is usually a good idea! Repeat these after your teacher ...

Give me that book!

Give me that book, please.

Don't put your feet on the chair!

Don't put your feet on the chair, please.

Think of a something you use and give instructions to a partner on how to use it. Here is an example ...

My electric saw

This is very useful, but be careful. Always wear good gloves and protective glasses. Charge the battery (if necessary), but unplug it before you start – don't use the saw with the battery attached to the charging cable! Hold the saw with both hands and press at the same time with both hands to start. When you cut a branch, saw half way, then cut a little on the other side in the same place so that the branch doesn't split.

(This saw is not electric!)

85. My life story (past simple verbs)

Schooldays: complete these sentences with a verb:

- I _____ to primary school at the age of …

- At the age of … I _____ to secondary school.

- I _____ for examinations in a lot of subjects.

- I _____ school/ I did not _____ school very much.

- I _____ school at the age of …

Review: The past simple Tense

Regular past tenses end in -ed

move → moved

like → liked

stay → stayed

If the verb ends in '-y', the past tense ends '-ied'

study → studied

Don't forget that for negatives and questions, you just need 'did' + verb

What is the past tense of these verbs?

- leave → _____

- go → _____

- stay → _____

- get → _____

- become → _____

The word 'get' has many uses: in your life story, you will probably need these

= *to obtain*: I got a job as a pharmacist, I got a degree in civil engineering, I got a promotion

With certain expressions, = *to become*: I got married, I got divorced,

152

But use 'become' with jobs: I became a hairdresser, I became a teacher, I became a lab technician.

What did you do after school?

Read about these four people:

Mario

I went to college and I studied to be an electrician. I left college at the age of 20 and got a job as an electrical assistant. Two years later I changed jobs and I worked in a company for 6 years. (I also got married while I was in this company). In 2016 I started to work as an independent electrician. My wife helped me with the administration. Now we have two children. In the future I hope to work as an electrician in the UK.

Gina

I left school at the age of 16. I did not go to college or university. I got a job as a shop assistant. I stayed there for four years, but I left when I became a mother. I stayed at home to look after my child for 5 years. Then I got another job in a warehouse, but I didn't like it.

Abdul

I was unemployed when I left school. It was difficult to find work. I went to college and studied more – mainly maths and sciences – but I stopped at the age of 19 because there were a lot of problems in my country. I moved to England last year. In the future I hope to study more to get a better job.

Irina

After school, I went to university and studied engineering for four years. I got a job in a company that designs software for industry. It was a good job and I was happy there for ten years. I got married but I don't have any children. I hope I can find a software job in the UK soon.

Who says this – Mario, Gina, Abdul or Maria?

1. "I could not find a job when I left school"
2. "I was 20 when I had my first child"
3. "After leaving school, I went to university"
4. "I hope to study more in the future"
5. "I was employed for 8 years, then I became self-employed"

Choose sentences that you can use to describe your life:

(To describe your qualifications and your job history:)

I _____ to college/university for ____ years.

I did not ____ to college or university.

I l____ college at the age of _____ .

I g_____ a job as a (secretary).

I w_____ in a bank for ____ years.

(To describe personal details:)

I g____ married in (2005).

I b_____ a mother/father at the age of ____.

I s____ at home to be with my baby for _____ months.

I h____ another child at the age of _____.

In (2022) I m_____ to England.

Use the ideas from the sentences above to talk about your life so far!

You can start most of your sentences with "I", but to add variety, sometimes you can start with the year:

In 1996, I went to university in Tripoli.

...or you can start the sentence with "At the age of___"

At the age of 26 I had my first child.

86. Did you have a nice holiday?

Can you find the right sentence from the box to fit after each of these questions?

Hello! How are you?

....

Did you have a nice holiday?

....

Where did you go exactly?

....

How long did the journey take?

....

What was the weather like?

....

Did you have any problems?

....

Where did you stay?

....

It sounds great. I hope I can go there one day!

Here are the sentences you need for the other half of the conversation:

- It was nice and hot most of the time.
- Not really. The queues were very long at the airport, but we didn't miss our flight.
- Fine thanks. A bit tired from travelling – we only got back yesterday.
- We stayed with friends
- We went to Lake Baloton in Hungary.
- It wasn't too long – about a two-hour flight from Birmingham to Budapest.
- Yes, thank you, we had a lovely time.

87. British history

Listen to the presentation* about English history and complete the text with the words underneath. There are five answers in the box that you do not need!

The Romans _____ Britain in 55 b.C. and occupied for about 400 years. After that, in the _____ period, there were several kingdoms, but when William of Normandy invaded in _____, he established a kingdom that covered most of England. His descendants have continued to occupy the throne, though there have been battles between different branches of the family. In the fifteenth century, there were the 'Wars of the _____'. The Tudor family ruled through the _____ century, followed by the Stuarts in the seventeenth century. There was _____ when there was no king after Parliamentarians under Oliver Cromwell overthrew the Stuart King Charles I, but his son, _____II, returned from exile to take up the throne after Cromwell's death. By this time, the monarch was increasingly obliged to accept the decisions of parliament, which was made clear in_____. We call Britain a 'constitutional monarchy'. The eighteenth century is known as the Georgian period as there were four King_____! Britain developed as an important world power, especially as its _____ was very strong. Large colonies were established, though the _____colonies gained independence in 1776. The industrial revolution was also important as Britain developed factories and there were great achievements in engineering. Queen Victoria reigned from 1837 to_____, and was the longest-serving monarch until she was recently overtaken by Queen _____II, who started to reign in 1952. In the twentieth century, Britain was engaged in the two world wars (1914-18 and 1939-45). It joined the European Community (later the European Union) in_____, but left after a referendum in 2016.

Roses	navy	invaded	1970	sixteenth	Anglo-Saxon	1066
Georges	a year	a decade	a century	1901	Elizabeth	
Charles	1688	army	American	Tulips	1980	

*Teacher's script on the next page

Teacher's script

The Romans, led by Julius Caesar, invaded Britain in 55 b.C. and occupied for about 400 years. After that there were several kingdoms, including areas governed by invading forces including Danes and Saxons. We call it the Anglo-Saxon period, and the most important kingdom was the kingdom of Wessex in the south. When William of Normandy invaded in 1066, he established a kingdom that covered most of England. His descendants have continued to occupy the throne, though there have been battles between different branches of the family. In the fifteenth century, for example, there were the 'Wars of the Roses' – the York branch of the family had a white rose as its symbol, the Lancaster branch had a red rose. Finally Henry Tudor, who became King Henry VII (the seventh), defeated the York King Richard III (the third) and brought to wars to an end, marrying Elizabeth of York. The Tudor family ruled through the sixteenth century, and included the infamous King Henry VIII {who had six wives!), and Queen Elizabeth I (the first). The Tudors were followed by the Stuarts in the seventeenth century. There was a decade when there was no king after Parliamentarians under Oliver Cromwell overthrew the Stuart King Charles I, but his son, Charles II, returned from exile to take up the throne after the death of the unpopular Cromwell. By this time, the monarch was increasingly obliged to accept the decisions of parliament, which was made clear in 1688. We call Britain a 'constitutional monarchy'. The eighteenth century is known as the Georgian period as there were four King Georges! Britain developed as an important world power, especially as its navy had been very strong since the time of Elizabeth I. Large colonies were established, though the American colonies gained independence in 1776. The industrial revolution was also important for Britain at this time. Industrialists developed factories and there were great achievements in engineering. Most of the nineteenth century is known as the Victorian age. Queen Victoria reigned from 1837 to 1901, and was the longest-serving monarch until she was recently overtaken by Queen Elizabeth II, who started to reign in 1952 and enjoyed a seventy-year reign. In the twentieth century, Britain was engaged in the two world wars (1914-18 and 1939-45), though it was never occupied by its enemies. After the second world war, European countries became closer economically and politically. Britain joined the European Community (later the European Union) in 1970, but, as the Union grew to nearly thirty countries in the early years of the twenty-first century, some British people were unhappy. As a result, Britain left after a referendum in 2016.

88. Roman numerals

Often clocks in Britain use these Roman numbers:

I = one

II = two

III = three

IV = four

V = five

VI = six

VII = seven

VIII = eight

IX = nine

X = ten

XI = eleven

XII = twelve

We also use them for kings and queens, so you see 'Charles III' but we say 'Charles the third'. One of the most famous kings was Henry the eighth, so you will see Henry VIII.

Look out for other Roman numerals, for example on monuments.

L = fifty

C = a hundred

M = a thousand

What do you think these numbers are? – XL, LXX, CXVII

Sometimes you see a year written in Roman numbers – Have fun trying to work them out!

89. Subject and object pronouns

subject	object
I	me
you	you
he/she/it	him/her/it
we	us
they	them

Subjects and objects

The subject normally comes before the verb and is the person (or thing) that does the verb. The object normally comes after the verb and receives the verb!

Subject	verb	Object
I	saw	a friend
We	learn	English
They	left	the hotel
David/he	bought	a car
The dog/It	attacked	me!

You can also use object pronouns after a preposition:

My friend will come **with me**.

Can you give it **to us**, please?

*A little exercise: replace the **names or things** with a pronoun*

Mr Smith writes to me sometimes → **He** writes to me sometimes

Alison likes **cricket** → **She** likes **it**.

1. **Ian** bought **a shirt** → _____ bought _____.
2. **My daughter** drinks **tea and coffee** → _____ drinks _____.
3. **Jim and Jackie** both like **curry** → _____ both like _____.
4. **I and my friend** visited **a museum** → _____ visited _____.
5. **Sarah** ate **some sweets** → _____ ate _____.

My brother wrote to **me and my wife**.

159

90. A polite conversation

(Passive verbs)

Some polite phrases:

That's very kind of you (*when someone offers you something*)

Never mind! (*something is not quite right but it's not very serious*)

It doesn't matter (*it's not serious, it's not very important*)

I'm afraid... (*You are sorry to say that...*)

That's a shame (*something is not right*)

I'm so sorry to hear that (*something quite serious is not right*)

If it's not too much trouble (*you ask for something but only if it is not difficult*)

Would you excuse me? (*you need to go!*)

Use one of these phrases for these situations:

- Someone gives you a present

- Someone tells you that a family member has died

- You want to say that you don't understand very well

- Someone tells you that it rained a lot during their holiday

- You would like a drink

- You are talking to someone but have to leave

Practise the conversation below in pairs...

Person A is the host, person B is a guest

    A. Good morning. My name is _____ _____

    B. Good morning Mr/Ms _____. My name is _____ _____

    A. I**'m pleased** to meet you Mr/Ms _____. Welcome!

    B. Here is a small gift. These biscuits **are made** in my country.

    A. Thank you, that's very kind.

B. I'm afraid some of them **are broken**

A. Oh, it doesn't matter.

B. My wife/husband is sorry she/he can't be with me. She/he **is needed** at home.

A. That's a shame. Never mind, I'**m delighted** you could come.

B. **Are** you **married**, Mr/Ms _____?

A. Yes, my wife/husband is over there serving the drinks. What would you like to drink?

B. I'll have a glass of water, please – hot water, if it's not too much trouble.

A. I'm sure that **can be arranged**. Let's go over to the drinks table...
   [introduces the visitor to his wife/husband] This is Mr/Ms _____.
   He would like a cup of hot water.

B. If it's not too much trouble. I'**m pleased** to meet you Mrs/Mr

   _____.

A. Would you excuse me? I have to greet some more guests.

B. Of course. Thank you for your welcome.

The verbs in bold have the verb 'to be' (am/is/are) + past participle: we call this **'passive'**, and it is used when the subject does not do the verb:

> **The biscuits are made** – 'the biscuits' are the subject, but someone else does the making!

> **She is needed at home** – 'She' is the subject, but someone else needs her!

> **I'm sure that can be arranged** – a combination of the modal 'can' and the passive.

Very often the past participle is like an adjective: **I'm married, I'm pleased, I'm delighted**. Is this a passive, or just 'to be' + an adjective? ... It doesn't matter!!!

91. Taking a train

Your teacher plays the part of a Railway Station Official. Listen to the conversation and note down the missing information:

Traveller: *Hello. I want to go from Rugby to Birmingham. When is the next train?*

Station Official: There is a train at ___ ___, then another one at ___ ___. That's a fast train, it only stops at Coventry.

- *What time does the first train arrive?*

- It gets into New Street at ___ ___. The second one arrives ___ minutes later.

- *I see. How much is it?*

- Single or return?

- *Return please. I will come back this evening.*

- First class or second class?

- *Second class (I can't afford first class!)*

- That's £__ ___ if you take the first train.

- *Is the price different for the second train?*

- The second train will be £__ ___. It's a different company.

- *I see. I will take the second train, please. Here you are!*

- Thank you, here's your ticket.

- *What platform is it?*

- Platform ___.

- *Thank you very much.*

Read the conversation with a partner: you can change the information on prices, times and the platform number. If you are the traveller, note down the information and check at the end that you have understood correctly.

Trains in Britain

There are several train companies who operate the trains in Britain. Because of this, there may be different prices for the same journey. You can sometimes save money by buying a ticket online in advance. You will normally need to scan or show your ticket before you can get onto a platform, but at small stations you may just board the train and show your ticket to an official on the train. In exceptional circumstances you can buy tickets on the train, but on most trains you have to pay a fine (a penalty) if you get on a train without a valid ticket.

Trains before 9.00 am are often more expensive. If you buy an "off-peak" ticket, this means you cannot use it at the busiest times. It can be quite complicated!

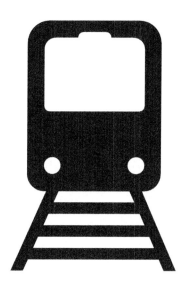

92. An excerpt from the novel "A Victorian Journey"

(past perfect tense)

In what century was the Victorian period? See the section on 'British History'.

George, Louise and Emma are servants for a wealthy family in London, the Pryces. Mrs Harris is the housekeeper, in charge of the young servants. Don't try to understand every word, but use a dictionary for some words so that you understand enough.

On a summer Saturday it was decided that the whole family would go for a walk and a picnic. The staff would accompany them to carry the lunch. Emma carried one crate with Mrs Harris, George and Louise another. The older boys were at home and the Reverend Pryce ordered two carriages to take them to the far east of London to Greenwich. The carriages dropped them at the bottom of a hill by the riverside and the party walked up into parkland to find a spot with a view of the city.

"So what are your ambitions?"

Louise was addressing the question to George as they carried their crate up the hill. He was taken aback by the question. In the past he **had asked** her a few questions about her family and her schooling, but he could not remember her asking him a question. He was slow to answer.

"I don't really know. I wanted to come to London because I didn't just want to work on the farm all my life."

"So what now? Are you just going to be a servant all your life?"

"No, no, I will find an occupation, just don't know what yet."

The family **had stopped** and were debating a position. Some wanted to be under trees, others were enjoying the warmth of the July sunshine. Mrs Pryce ordered the staff to set up the picnic under some trees.

Any observer of the scene would clearly see who were the servants in this party of ten. The Pryces ate, drank, played and conversed, while George, Emma, Louise and Mrs Harris stood silently to the sides waiting to respond to any request. They themselves neither ate nor drank until the master signalled to Mrs Harris that they should take some food for themselves, at which point she gathered some of the leftovers onto a couple of plates and passed them around the servants.

(from *A Victorian Journey* by Ian Sydenham, available on amazon.co.uk)

Some questions on the text

1. What season was it?
2. What day of the week was it?
3. What month was it?
4. How did they travel to Greenwich?
5. What did George do before he came to London?
6. Where did they set up the picnic?

If you like drawing, you could try to draw a picture of the picnic party!

Read the conversation between George and Louise – here it is again:

> *"So what are your ambitions?"*
>
> *"I don't really know. I wanted to come to London because I didn't just want to work on the farm all my life."*
>
> *"So what now? Are you just going to be a servant all your life?"*
>
> *"No, no, I will find an occupation, just don't know what yet."*

Now you answer the question "What are your ambitions?"

Verbs

Can you see which words in the text are verbs? Most of the verbs are past simple verbs, with the regular form ending -ed. Which irregular verbs are in the text? Can you find any examples of passive verbs?

Past perfect tense - had + past participle (there are two examples in the text in bold type).

had asked- George asked questions before this conversation took place.

had stopped – Before George said "No, no, I will find an occupation…" the family stopped walking.

The past perfect – 'had + past participle'

Used when we add a sentence that is even more past than the rest of our sentences! Look at these examples:

1. *I went to the shops but I could not buy anything because I **had left** my bank card at home.*

   The chronological order is this:

   - I left my bank card at home.

   - I went to the shops.

   - I could not buy anything.

2. *I had to take a test about British history. Fortunately my English teacher **had told** us some things and I was able to answer most of the questions.*

   The chronological order is this:

   - My English teacher told us some things about British history.

   -I had to take a test.

   -I was able to answer most of the questions.

Now put the first sentence here to the end – you will need to change it to past perfect!

   I did not sign the form

   I sent the form to the Town Hall,

   but they returned it to me because...

93. Lost property

Read this conversation with a partner:

Official: Can I help you?

Other person: Good morning/afternoon. I've lost my phone and wondered if someone has handed it in.

Official: I see. Can you describe it?

Other person: It's a smartphone... it's a _____ [*manufacturer*]... It's black/red/white... It has a case that opens like a book.

Official: I'll have a look for you [*gets out a box of phones*!] Can you tell me the number please?

Other person: Yes it's 09876 54321

Official [*repeats the number and types it into his/her phone*]: 09876 54321

Other person [*a phone in the box rings!!*]: Ah, great, it's there!

Official: Yes, you're lucky! Here it is. I need to take some details please. Can I have your name please?

Other person: _____ _____

Official: and your postcode?

Other person: __ __ __ __ __ __

Official: Thank you. And the house name or number?

Other person: __ __ __

Official: Thank you. Could you sign here, please, to confirm that I have given you the phone?

Other person: Certainly. Thank you so much. Do I have to pay anything?

Official: No, but you can put a couple of coins in our charity box if you like. Here's your phone!

Other person: Wonderful. It's such a relief! Thank you again, Goodbye!

Official: You're welcome! Goodbye

1. *Read the conversation again but change some of the details.*

2. *Now use the conversation to describe something different: a bag, a watch, a jacket. In the middle of the conversation, miss out the part where the official rings the phone – just have the official say "I'll have a look... Yes, you're lucky! Here it is!"*

3. *Can you change the end of the conversation because the official doesn't have the lost item? He/she will still want to note details so that he/she can contact the person if the item is found.*

Review: The present perfect tense

The present perfect tense (have + past participle) is normally used because something started in the past and continues in the present:

How long have you lived in Rugby? I have been here for six months.

Sometimes it is used for something very recent, only just completed. There are a couple of examples of this in the conversation about lost property:

*"I h**ave lost** my phone"*

(Very recent, and the situation continues to preoccupy the person. Contrast this sentence: "When I was on holiday last year, I lost my phone")

*"Could you sign here, please, to confirm that I **have given** you the phone?"*

(Very recent!)

Look at the last paragraph of the text about the European Union in Unit 107. Can you find examples of the present perfect tense used for recent events?

The other use of this tense is to describe experiences which may be repeated in the future:

What jobs have you done in the past? I have been an office worker, I have worked in a warehouse and I have helped my parents with the family business.

The list of irregular verbs on the next page is not a full list, but it gives you some of the most frequent verbs to learn. As you can see, the past participle is often the same as the past simple tense.

Present verb	Past simple	Past participle
am/is /are (to be)	was/were	been
do/does	did	done
have	had	had
go	went	gone
see	saw	seen
come	came	come
speak	spoke	spoken
eat	ate	eaten
drink	drank	drunk
sleep	slept	slept
(under)stand	(under)stood)	(under)stood
(for)get	(for)got	(for)got/forgotten
lose	lost	lost
give	gave	given
know	knew	known
read	read ['red']	read ['red']
take	took	taken
tell	told	told
say	said ['sed']	said ['sed']
make	made	made
send	sent	sent
leave	left	left
hear	heard	heard
buy	bought	bought
sing	sang	sung
ring	rang	rung
bring	brought	brought
meet	met	met
grow	grew	grown

Negatives and questions

For the present simple and past simple, you use 'do/does/did' to make questions and negatives (except for the verb 'to be' and modal verbs). For structures using the past participle (Present Perfect, Past Perfect and Passives) there is no 'do/does/did' in negatives and questions.
Have you been here long? I wasn't told about your arrival. Sorry, I haven't had time to make a cup of coffee. Were you met at the station?

94. Our planet is dying!

The Present Continuous (or Present Progressive) tense is used for what is happening **at the moment**, so it is used in this text about today's environmental problems.

Read the text, look for examples of the Present Continuous, then answer the questions at the end.

The climate is changing. Average temperatures are rising everywhere, with the result that polar ice-caps are melting. This means that there is an increased risk of flooding. There have been more forest fires, which adds to the problem of deforestation – we have been chopping down trees and the global air quality has been damaged. Droughts are more frequent and crop failure means famine for many throughout the world. Pollution is affecting our waters as well as our air. There can be little doubt that human beings are responsible for global warming, pollution and deforestation.

What can we do to preserve the planet for our children and grandchildren? Some action needs to be taken at a global level, so governments have to work together to reduce dependence on fossil fuels, to stop the destruction of trees and to punish those who continue to pollute the atmosphere and the waterways. The development of renewable energy sources is a major priority. As individuals, we need to recycle as much as possible, to reduce our energy consumption, especially when we are using fossil fuels, and we may need to change some of our eating habits. Eating locally-produced food is preferable to eating foods that need to be transported from other parts of the world. We may need to reduce our meat consumption as cattle and some other animals contribute to pollution levels, especially where there is an abnormal concentration of animals. Plastic is dangerous because it will not decompose. It ends up in our rivers and seas, where particles are eaten by fish and other sea creatures. We all need therefore to reduce our use of plastic.

Questions – answer these questions using the information in the text

1. Give two examples of things damaging the quality of the air.
2. What cause of famine does the author mention?

3. Can you give some examples of 'fossil fuels'.
4. Who should be punished?
5. Why is it good to eat locally-produced food?
6. Why is plastic more dangerous than paper?
7. Can you give some examples of 'renewable energy'?
8. Why should we reduce our consumption of meat?

Now try to fill in this table. You can add to the ideas in the text with your own ideas. Some examples have been filled in for you.

Problem	Cause	Action needed	By?
Forest fires			Governments
Drought			
Plastic in rivers and seas			
Global warming	Use of fossil fuels		
Cattle pollution		Reduce our meat consumption	

What's your opinion?

Talk about the environmental problems with other people. You could start...

In my opinion the biggest problem is...

People should...

Governments should...

95. More modal verbs: shall, should, ought to

Read this conversation:

How are you today?

- *Not too good.*

What's the matter?

- *I have a high temperature. I didn't sleep well.*

Oh dear. Maybe you **should** see the doctor.

- *I don't know. Maybe I'll wait 24 hours.*

Shall I make you an appointment? You can cancel it if you feel better.

- *Ok, that's kind of you.*

You **ought to** lie down and rest. I'll call the doctor's surgery...

*These modal verbs are not so frequent as **can/may/must/will**, but you **should** know them*

*'**should**' and '**ought to**' are very similar in meaning: we use them for suggestions and advice. If you want to be stronger, use **must**:*

"You should see a doctor" (or "You ought to see a doctor") – I advise you to see a doctor, I think it is a good idea

"You must see a doctor" – it is very important that you see a doctor, I order it!

Sometimes '**should**' is advice to yourself!

"I shouldn't drink alcohol – I have to drive later."

Like the other modal verbs, we don't use "do/does" for negatives and questions:

Should I take my passport with me? (What do you advise?)

- *No, I shouldn't. You won't need it.* (won't = will not)

'shall' is often used in questions as in the example above "Shall I make you an appointment?" and means '**Would you like me/us to...**'

Shall I make a cup of tea? Shall we go shopping tomorrow?

(Sometimes 'shall' is simply an alternative to 'will' for the future, but in most cases it is easier to use 'will').

Here is another conversation: which word fits in the spaces? (Sometimes there are two possibilities).

Would you like a cup of tea or coffee?

- *No thank you.*

_____ I get you a glass of water?

- *Yes, that would be nice. Thank you.*

We _____ celebrate your arrival. _____ I open a bottle of wine?

- *No thank you. I _____ not drink alcohol because of my medication.*

I see. We _____ to do something. _____ I get you a piece of cake?

- *Thank you, I will have a piece of cake with my glass of water.*

96. The British Isles, the United Kingdom, Britain, England etc.

It can be confusing that sometimes people in Britain refer to their country in several different ways. This text explains what is meant by the various terms.

The two large islands situated north-west of France are called the **British Isles**. The larger of the two is called **Great Britain**, and consists of three countries – **England, Scotland and Wales**. Scotland is to the north, Wales is in the west, and the largest of the three is England – most of the south of the island.

Because of its geography, **Wales** has historically been separate from England, but since 1536 it has been joined to England for political purposes. It has an assembly in the capital, Cardiff, but the Welsh people also elect Members of Parliament (MPs) to the Westminster House of Commons in London.

Scotland was also historically separate from England. When the Romans invaded Britain from 55 b.C., they stopped at a point marked by 'Hadrian's Wall', some of which still stands today. North of this border, Scotland was a separate country, but in 1603 the King of Scotland became King of England as well (because he was a descendant of King Henry VIII of England, and Queen Elizabeth I died in 1603 without children). It was only in 1707 that England and Scotland officially agreed to become one nation. Today there is a separate parliament in Edinburgh (the capital of Scotland), which has greater powers than the Welsh Assembly but the people of Scotland also elect MPs to the London Parliament in Westminster.

Ireland (the island to the west) has at times been governed by the English monarchs, but after a struggle for independence in the early years of the twentieth century, most of the island became the Republic of Ireland, also known as Eire. The Irish Free State Constitution Act of 1922 recognises the independence of Ireland, but the north-east of the island chose to remain attached to Great Britain and continue to be governed from Westminster. This part is normally referred to as Northern Ireland.

The United Kingdom of Great Britain and Northern Ireland therefore consists of four nations – England, Scotland, Wales and Northern Ireland. Politically they are all under the authority of the Westminster Parliament, but they operate as separate nations in many respects, for example, in sports like football where each has its own national team.

When Britain left the European Union after the 'Brexit' referendum of 2016, the border between Northern Ireland and the Republic of Ireland became a land border between the UK and the European Union. This has caused some problems as there were no border controls between Northern Ireland and the Republic.

People of the United Kingdom of Great Britain and Northern Ireland will normally refer to themselves as 'British', but they may use 'English', 'Scottish', 'Welsh' or 'Irish'.

Can you label the map of the British Isles with these names?

Great Britain	England	Wales	Scotland	Northern Ireland
The Republic of Ireland				

Try to simply explain to another person what each name refers to!

97. Monarchy vs republic

Read the text below, then have a discussion...

Britain has what is known as 'a constitutional monarchy'. The King or Queen has limited powers, while real political power rests with the Parliament.
The parliament is divided into two chambers – The House of Commons and the House of Lords. The House of Commons is democratically elected, though the members of the House of Lords are chosen in a variety of ways, not directly elected by the people. For this reason the power of the House of Lords is limited to amending the proposals of the House of Commons and sending them back, after which the House of Commons can decide whether or not to accept the suggestions of the Lords. Every Act of Parliament is passed to the monarch for signature, but this is a formality.
One curious tradition is the State Opening of Parliament, when the monarch speaks to the Parliament, but the words he speaks are written by the Prime Minister and the government!
Many love the British system, and the monarchy is followed around the world. People love the pageantry – processions, royal robes, traditional rituals – but the monarchy has its opponents. Some say that it is unfair, that these unelected members of the royal family have wealth and influence simply because they were born into this family. Supporters of turning Britain into a republic argue that people should always have the possibility to change their government in an election if they are unhappy with it, but the royal family are in their position for the whole of their lives.
Whether the royal family is expensive for the British people is a subject of controversy. While there is an obvious cost to the British taxpayer to support the royals, the country also earns money through the international interest that the royal family brings, notably in tourism. The royal family (particularly the monarch) provides a useful 'neutral' head of state who does not change as often as politicians and can welcome international visitors without having a political background.

No doubt the debate will continue as to whether the British royal family should maintain its role in public life.

What do you think? Do you think it is good to have a king or queen? Make a list of some of the advantages and disadvantages, then have a discussion with your class, or with another person.

Advantages	Disadvantages
The person does not change every four years.	It can be expensive.

Here are some questions to ask a British person...

Do you like the royal family?

Do you think it is a good thing to have a king or queen?

Is it very expensive for the country?

What do you think of the present monarch?

Would it be better to have an elected head of state?

Have you ever met a member of the royal family?

It may be difficult for you to talk about the situation in your home country, but if possible, describe its government, whether it is a republic or a monarchy or some other form of government. Keep it simple! There is another chapter later in this book with more detail about elections in Britain.

98. Conversation: More slowly, please!

(Adverbs)

Read the conversation between a local person and a person from overseas:

Local person: Hello! How are you?

Person from overseas: Fine thank you, and you?

LP: Not too bad. It's **really** cold today.

Pfo: Yes, we need a lot of warm clothes.

LP: **Absolutely**! Are you going to the fireworks on Saturday?

Pfo: Sorry, can you repeat that more slowly, please?

LP: The fireworks, on Saturday? Do you know about that?

Pfo: No, I don't know about that. Where are the fireworks?

LP: In the park. It's usually very good. I bought some tickets, but I **stupidly** lost them. So I bought some more and now I've found the others. Would you like to have them?

Pfo: I'm sorry, I didn't understand. Could you say it again, please?

LP: Certainly, I'll try to speak more **slowly**! I have three tickets for the fireworks. Would you like them? I don't want any money for them.

Pfo: Thank you! That's very kind of you.

LP: Here are the tickets. Look after them **carefully**!

Pfo: Will your husband be there?

LP: No, he's **extremely** busy at the moment. It will just be me and the children.

Pfo: I see. Thank you again! Goodbye!

LP: Goodbye! See you on Saturday.

*What do you notice about the words in **bold** type? These words are **adverbs**. Read the notes on the next page.*

Some notes about adverbs:

1. We usually form adverbs by adding -ly to an adjective:

adjective	*adverb*
careful	carefully
slow	slowly
usual	usually
extreme	extremely
certain	certainly
good	well

2. An adjective describes a noun, and an adverb describes the verb: *Can you speak slowly, please?* – the adverb 'slowly' goes with the verb 'speak'

3. Some adverbs are used as a one-word sentence, normally to express that you agree! *Absolutely! Certainly! Totally!*

4. 'really' and 'extremely' are often used as an alternative to 'very': *He's extremely busy = He's very busy.*

5. The position of an adverb varies:

- sometimes we put them at the beginning (as in this sentence – '*sometimes* is an adverb!). This is usually the position for '*Fortunately*' *and 'Unfortunately'.*

- adverbs of frequency (*always, often, usually, normally, generally, sometimes, rarely, never*) often come before the verb: *He usually arrives late. My wife never wears skirts.* (but after the verb 'to be': *I am always pleased to see you*!)

- other adverbs may also come before the verb ('*I stupidly lost them'*) or after the verb as in '*Can you speak slowly, please*?' You will need to listen and observe how they are used and copy what you hear and see!

Can you insert some adverbs into this speech?

Hello! I'm ___ pleased to see you. I will speak _____, but if you don't understand me, please raise your hand. Please write your name _____ on the name cards. We _____ use first names in these meetings. I need to give some safety instructions, so please listen _____.

99. Looking for accommodation

Conversation at an estate agent's office

Do you know the words for rooms in a house or an apartment? Check the meaning of these words:

A bedroom   a kitchen   a living room/a lounge   a dining room   a cellar
a bathroom   a utility room   a shower room   an en-suite a study
a balcony   a garden   a hallway   a staircase   a cloakroom

Listen to your teacher and his/her helper reading the conversation. What do they say in the spaces?

Estate agent: Good _____1._____ How can I help you?

Client: We're looking for an apartment, and I saw an advert for a place in Rose Crescent

Estate agent: Oh yes, that's a _____2._____ bedroomed flat. Is that what you are looking for?

Client: Yes, possibly. Can you tell us more about it?

Estate Agent: Let me see... It has a _____3._____ room, a kitchen and the bedrooms. And a bathroom.

Client: Does the bathroom have a bath or a shower?

Estate Agent: It has a _____4._____.

Client: How much is it?

Estate Agent: It's _____5._____ per month.

Client: I see. Do you have anything similar at a lower price?

Estate Agent: Yes, I think we have a couple of others. There's one here that's a bit less, still the same number of bedrooms.

Client: Where is that?

Estate Agent: In the town centre, _____6._____Road.

Client: What are the schools like in that area?

Estate Agent: To be honest, the schools near Rose Crescent have a better reputation, which may be why the price is higher, but there are some good schools in the town centre too.

Client: Could we make an appointment to see the cheaper flat ?

Estate Agent: Certainly. My colleague will make you an appointment. He's just speaking to another client at the moment. Would you like to take a seat? ...

Client: Thank you.

When you have checked the missing words, read the conversation with a partner.

Review: The present continuous (or present progressive) tense

There are a couple of examples of this in the conversation:

We're looking for an apartment.

He's just speaking to another client at the moment.

1. This tense is used for something that is happening now, at the moment.

What are you doing? We're looking for an apartment!

Where are you going? I'm going to an estate agent's.

The form of this tense is to use **am/is/are + verb ending -ing**

2. Sometimes it is used for a near future, as in this conversation:
- Do you have any plans for the weekend?
- Not much. I'm going shopping on Saturday, and on Sunday I think my sister is coming to see us.

Don't over-use this tense – it is not as frequent as the ordinary present tense.

100. The future of energy

Here is another text for you to read and discuss:

Fossil fuels such as coal and gas are responsible for much of the pollution that is causing global warming. Scientific advances are finding some new ways of providing energy.

Renewable energy such as solar power and wind power is providing much more electricity than a generation ago. Wind farms are a common sight in Britain, though many people don't like huge wind turbines spoiling the view of the countryside. A popular solution is to position wind turbines in the sea, and much of the British coastline is now surrounded by wind farms – hundreds of wind turbines providing a source of energy that does not pollute the atmosphere. Solar panels are now widespread too, both on private housing and on larger buildings.

Nuclear power is preferred in some countries as the solution to our energy needs. France has invested heavily in nuclear energy, while Germany has seen a lot of resistance to it. There is concern about the danger of a nuclear accident, and the disposal of waste is another issue that provokes opposition. Recent progress in nuclear fusion could provide a future energy source, and in some areas hydro-electric plants are using water to produce electricity.

Then of course there are cars – a major contributor to poor air quality in our cities. Electric cars are now commonplace, and in the next twenty years we may say goodbye to petrol-driven vehicles. Improved storage in batteries makes it possible to drive longer distances between charging, and the latest battery technology may also help us to power our homes with renewable energy sources such as wind and solar.

Understanding the text

Explain these words to another person:

renewable

widespread

resistance

improved

solution

Now complete this shorter text (you may need more than one word):

Examples of fossil fuels are _____ and _____.

Examples of renewable energy sources are _____ and _____.

Some countries are unsure about the safety of _____ energy.

In the future, most cars will be _____.

In Britain, a popular location for wind turbines is _____.

Verbs in the text: identify the tense of these verbs: choose from

Present simple   Present Perfect   Present Continuous   Present Passive

verb	tense
don't like	
is providing	
has invested	
is preferred	

Verbs ending in **-ing**

As well as after the verb "like" (*I like cycling, I don't like swimming*), and with Present Continuous verbs, you will find verbs ending -**ing** in sentences – here are two examples from the text "The Future of Energy":

*People don't like huge wind turbines **spoiling** the view of the countryside.*

*... hundreds of wind turbines **providing** a source of energy.*

We use -**ing** to join the two ideas together. We can also use the word "**which**" in these sentence and the meaning is exactly the same:

*People don't like huge wind turbines **which spoil** the view of the countryside.*

*... hundreds of wind turbines **which provide** a source of energy.*

Look out for more examples of this as you hear and read more English. We will return to the use of '**which**' in a later chapter.

101. Phrasal verbs

Many expressions have a combination of a verb with another word to give a new meaning – we call them phrasal verbs. Here are some common phrasal verbs:

To wake up = to stop sleeping

To get up = to get out of bed, to leave your bed

To pick up = to give someone a lift in a car (also = to take something in your hand)

To turn on = to start a machine (e.g. the light)

To turn off = to stop a machine

(*to switch on / to switch off* are very similar)

To get on (a bus) = to enter (the bus)

To get off (a train) = to leave (the train)

To get in (a car) = to enter (the car)

To get out of (a car) = to leave the car

To get rid of = to dispose of, to throw away

There are a lot of these phrases – try to learn a few of them and note new ones when you hear or see them. What makes sense in this conversation?

An English friend sees you on the street and stops the car to talk to you:

- *Hello. Where do you want to go?*
- To the shops in the town centre.
- *__ __ the car, I'll drop you near the shops.*
- Thank you! I woke ___ late this morning and I think I missed the bus.
- *No problem. I'll be about an hour in town. Would you like me to ___ you __ and bring you back here?*
- That's very kind, but I can get a bus back.
- *We're nearly there. If you ___ ___ of the car here, the shops are just on the left.*
- Thank you again. Have a nice day!

102. The National Health Service

Read the text about the National Health Service, then complete the summary below.

The National Health Service (normally referred to as the NHS), is the public health care system in England, covering hospitals, doctors and other key medical services. It is funded by the taxpayer and most of its services are provided free to users (provided the user is registered with an NHS number).

The NHS was set up following the second world war and started to function in 1948. There is a parallel private healthcare sector, used by approximately 8% of the population and funded mostly through private medical insurance. The private sector can sometimes offer quicker treatment or greater comfort in its hospitals, but it is probably most important in the area of dentistry, which is only partially supported by the NHS.

Anyone can register with a doctor. Local doctors are normally referred to as 'GPs' ('General Practitioners) and are based at a 'surgery' in cities, towns and sometimes in larger villages. You normally need an appointment to see a doctor, so if you need emergency treatment, you may have to go to a hospital. Look for signs to 'A and E' – Accident and Emergency. Some towns also have a 'walk-in' centre for minor emergencies.

Registration with a dentist can be more difficult. Many dentists say that they cannot take any more NHS patients. Private treatment is usually more expensive than NHS treatment, and some dental treatment is free on the NHS, for example for children under the age of 18.

If you are prescribed medicine by the doctor, you take a prescription to a pharmacy (or chemist's). There is a fixed charge for prescriptions, but people in certain categories can get free prescriptions.

Complete this text: some answers are just letters of the alphabet!

The health service in England is normally called the ___ ____ ____.

If you have a medical problem, you contact the __ ___ surgery to make an appointment with a doctor.

In an emergency, you may need to go to the ___ and ___ department at the local hospital.

If the doctor wants you to take some medicine, he will give you a _____ to take to a chemist's (or _____).

Dental treatment is not normally free, but it is less expensive on the NHS than with a _____ dentist.

Conversation: calling the dentist

Listen to the conversation as your teacher and a volunteer read it, and fill in the gaps.

Dentist's surgery: Black's dental surgery, how can I help you?

Patient: Hello. I need to see a dentist. I have _____(1.)_____

DS: I see. Are you registered with us?

P: No, I moved here recently.

DS: I'm afraid we're not taking on any new NHS _____ (2.)___. Are you happy to make an appointment for private treatment?

P: Is it very expensive?

DS: Well, it depends on the treatment you need. A check-up costs £__(3.)_, and a typical filling costs £__ (4)___. Most patients take out a care plan and pay monthly.

P: I see. Do you know any dentists here who will treat me on the __ (5)___?

DS: I can't give information about other_____(6)._____, but if you search online it may tell you if a dentist is taking on new NHS patients.

P: Thank you for help. I will see if I can find an NHS dentist first.

DS: That's fine. Good luck!

103. Conversation in the park (first conditional)

You meet a friend in the park... Read the conversation with a partner.

You: Hello, how are you?

Friend: Fine thanks, and you?

You: I'm OK, thanks. Do you often come here?

Friend: If the children aren't in school, we come here most days.

You: It's a nice day, today.

Friend: Yes. It's a bit cold, but at least it's not raining.

You: Will you be here tomorrow? I have a book to give you.

Friend: We'll be here if it doesn't rain, but I think the forecast isn't good.

You: I see. If it rains, I won't be here, but if it's not raining I will bring the book here, and if I see you, I will give it to you.

Friend: OK, thank you. I'll see you tomorrow then – if it doesn't rain!

Notice the way we use "if" in these sentences:

We'll be here if it doesn't rain. If it rains, I won't (=will not) be here.

The sentence has two parts – we call them clauses:

- The "if" clause – the part of the sentence with "if"
- The main clause – the other half of the sentence

In the examples, the "if" clause has a present tense, and the main clause has the future "will" + verb. There is also an example with the present continuous:

If it's not raining, I will bring the book here.

Textbooks often call this the "first conditional" – in later units we will see more complicated "if" clauses, sometimes called the second and third conditional.

Look at this sentence from the conversation. How is this different from the "first conditional" sentences?

If the children aren't in school, we come here most days.

Answer: the verb in the main clause is also in the present tense because it describes something that is generally the case, not something future. This is sometimes called the "zero conditional". It's not really conditional – we can replace the word "if" with "when" and it means the same.

When (or "if") the children have school, I do my shopping in the morning.

Now change the conversation: You meet your friend in the supermarket on a day when his/her children are in school. Try to include these sentences:

I do my shopping in the morning if the children are at school.

If the weather is nice at the weekend, we will go to Draycote Water.

If I see you, I will give you a brochure about Draycote Water.

(Sometimes the "if" clause comes first, sometimes the main clause comes first)

-

104. An accident (The past continuous tense)

The Past Continuous (also called the Past Progressive) is like the Present Continuous: It describes what was happening **at the moment** that something else happened. It often sets the scene for what follows.

Formation:

Was/were verb+ing

I was washing my hair when the phone rang.

We were watching a film when the fire alarm sounded.

Look for the examples of the past continuous in this conversation between a policeman and the witness of an accident:

Policeman: So, you saw the accident, is that right?

Witness: Yes officer.

Policeman: What were you doing?

Witness: I was waiting for a bus at the bus stop.

Policeman: Could you please describe what you saw?

Witness: The child was playing with a ball when the ball went into the road. He followed the ball into the road just as the car was coming round the corner.

Policeman: Was the car going too fast?

Witness: I'm not sure. To be honest, I was looking at my phone. I looked up when I heard the screech of brakes.

Policeman: Was it raining at the time?

Witness: No, I don't think so.

Policeman: I see. So did you see the moment that the car hit the child?

Witness: Yes – it was terrible. I hope he's all right.

Policeman: We don't think he has serious injuries, but the ambulance is taking him to hospital to check. What about the car that was coming in the other direction?

Witness: It swerved when it saw the child and crashed into a lamppost!

Policeman: Thank you for your help. In case we need them, can I note your name and contact details please?

Witness: Yes it's _____ _____ and my mobile number is _____.

Read the conversation in pairs, then try to draw a picture of the accident.

Talk about your day yesterday, and try to include three of these sentences:

The sun was shining.

It was raining.

I was relaxing in my room.

My friends were playing football.

What were you doing when the rain started?

The workmen were making a lot of noise.

As with the present continuous, don't use it too much! It's not as important as the simple past tense!

105. The British political system

The United Kingdom of Great Britain and Northern Ireland is governed centrally from Westminster, London, but there are also separate parliaments or assemblies in Scotland, Wales and Northern Ireland. Local councils decide on local issues. All of these bodies are elected by the population over the age of 18.

The official head of state is the monarch (king or queen), but he or she does not have any real political power. The power of the monarch has declined over the centuries and today the government is in the hands of the Westminster Parliament.

There are two houses (or chambers) – the House of Commons and the House of Lords. The House of Commons has the democratic authority as it is elected by the people, with a maximum term of five years. The House of Lords is not directly elected and therefore has only a limited power, but it can ask the House of Commons to review, revise or change in some way the new laws that it seeks to pass.

The Prime Minister is the leader of the party that wins the most seats in the House of Commons. Elections are based on constituencies – local geographical areas that each elect a member of Parliament. There are 650 seats in the House of Commons. The Prime Minister chooses members for a small governing council, called the Cabinet.

For many years, the two main parties have been the Conservative Party and the Labour Party. Smaller parties include the Liberal Democrats, the Green Party, and parties in Scotland, Wales and Northern Ireland that only represent people from those areas. At the moment in 2022, for example, the third biggest party in the House of Commons is the Scottish Nationalist Party. The Conservatives are the biggest party.

Complete the sentences from the box below:

The official head of state is the _____(1) but the political authority lies with the Parliament. The leader of the biggest party in the House of _____ (2) becomes the _____ _____(3) . Elections are normally held every _____ (4) years. The _____ (5) is a smaller group chosen by the Prime Minister to govern. The members of Parliament each represent a geographical area called a _____(6).

Cabinet	Prime Minister	five	constituency	Commons	monarch

What can you say about the system in your country?

Discuss with a partner the good things about the British system, and what things are not so good!

106. Reading a more difficult text

(Revision: Passive verbs)

If you try to read a text on a website, in a newspaper or in a magazine, don't worry if you don't understand everything! Which words can you understand? Can you understand enough to have an idea what the text is saying? Use a dictionary to check the meaning of an important word, but it is not normally necessary to translate everything into your own language – it takes a long time and you will not be able to read so much.

On the next few pages is a text describing the history of the European Union. Before you read it, here is another verb review.

Review: Passive verbs

With a passive verb, the object becomes the subject:

The dog chased the cat (active verb)

The cat was chased by the dog (passive verb)

We often use the passive because it is not so important who does the verb – the focus is on the person (or thing) receiving the verb:

59 people were injured.

The economic power of the EU can be considered greater than that of the United States.*

The passive tenses are formed with the verb 'to be' (*am/is/are* in the present tense, *was/were* in the past tense) + a past participle.

With regular verbs the past participle is the same as the past simple tense and ends -*ed*.

I am interested in history.

We are trapped!

With irregular verbs, you need to check the past participle (See page 61).

In the sentence marked*, the modal verb 'can' has been used with the passive, in which case 'be' is used. Here is another example:

You will be met at the station by Robert Smith.

Now here is a longer text with several examples of the passive highlighted:

*Draycote Water **is managed** by Severn Trent Water. Water **is drawn** from the River Leam and **treated** before it **is pumped** into the water supply for Rugby and the surrounding area. About fifty people **are employed** on the site to manage the leisure facilities, which include a café and a fishing centre. There is a sailing club which **is run** independently.*

So why do we use the passive?

- *Consider how the person or thing doing the verb is not as important as the person or thing receiving the verb:*
- *"Water is pumped" – it's not important who does the pumping!*
- *"I was born in 1958" – this is actually a passive, the verb "to bear"*

Can you complete these texts?

- *Text A*
  The sport of rugby ___1____ played in many countries, mostly in Europe and Oceania. Points ___2___ scored by carrying the ball across the other team's line or by kicking the ball between the posts. The ball must ____3___ passed backwards.
- *Text B*
  I ___4___ educated at a school in London and at the University of Bristol. My parents ___5___ employed in the health service. Before moving here I lived in Essex. I ___6____ interested in history and politics.

And finally...

> *Wife:* Other husbands do more housework than you!
> *Husband:* Can we change the subject?
> *Wife:* OK. Housework is done more by other husbands than by you!

As you read the text about the European Union, look for more examples of the passive...

107. The European Union

The European Union today has 27 member states. About 450 million people are part of EU countries and there are 24 official languages of member states. Moreover, the economic power of the EU can be considered greater than that of the United States and it is the largest trader in the world.

The Union has evolved over the last 60 years with countries joining on a voluntary basis. In 1957 six countries – France, West Germany, Italy, Belgium, the Netherlands and Luxembourg - signed the Treaty of Rome to form an economic community, the Common Market. The United Kingdom joined in 1973, along with Denmark and Ireland. A further wave of new members followed in the 1980s (Greece in '81, Spain and Portugal in '86).

There were major developments in the 1990s as the European Economic Community strengthened its cooperation even further by doing away with border controls and allowing the free movement of goods, money, people and services (The Schengen agreement of 1985, fully implemented by the Treaty of Maastricht in 1992). The "European Union" became the accepted title of the group of nations. Austria, Sweden and Finland joined in 1995. The member states accepted a common policy on many social laws and there was a growing assumption that the Union was moving towards a "United States of Europe"

Meanwhile, the turmoil in Eastern Europe meant that new states were queuing up to join. East Germany was automatically a member from the re-unification of Germany in 1990, and the collapse of Communism and the break-up of the Soviet Union left countries in the former Warsaw pact keen to join with the prosperous western countries of the EU. Several became members in 2004, then Romania and Bulgaria joined in 2007. The most recent addition was Croatia in 2013.

In 2002 most member countries adopted the Euro as a common currency. Not for the first time, the United Kingdom did not sign up to this. Britain had refused to do away with border controls in the 1992 Treaty, and had also refused to accept some of the social legislation adopted by the other member countries. As Europe expanded eastwards, the arrival of increasing numbers of workers from Eastern Europe in the wealthier countries of Germany, France and Britain caused some tensions, especially in the UK.

As global financial markets crashed in the closing years of the first decade of the twenty-first century, the Euro was under great pressure. The differences between the wealthier stronger economies, notably Germany, and the weaker struggling economies (in particular, Greece) were felt by many to be too significant for the same currency to be used by both extremes. Anti-EU feelings were becoming more noticeable in some countries.

In June 2016, Britain voted in a referendum to leave the EU. No other country has left the Union, and we are therefore in new territory. The Eurozone has stabilised, the Greek crisis has been managed, at least for the moment, though the economic weakness of several member countries may lead to further tensions in the future. In 2022, Britain has now left the Union but there are about eight new candidate countries hoping to join.

The European Union: Complete the text with the missing words.

The European Union today has ___ members. In 1957, ___ countries signed the first agreement, the Treaty of ____. The agreement was principally a trade deal, and the community was known as the _____ Market, or the EEC (European Economic Community). In 1973 three more countries joined, including the _____ _____. Spain and Portugal joined in _____.

With the Treaty of _____ in 1992, the closer ties between the member states were recognised by the use of the name "European Union". The Schengen agreement meant the removal of _____ _____, though Britain would not agree to this.

In _____ the single currency, the Euro, was adopted by most member states. Several countries from _____ Europe joined in the early years of the twenty-first century, following the collapse of the Warsaw Pact in the final years of the last century. The most recent addition was _____ in 2013. Several countries are candidates to join.

Britain, however, voted to leave the EU in _____ 2016 and is no longer a member.

1. Practise reading the summary you have just completed. You might like to add stress marks to help you pronounce it well.
   Some stress rules:
   a. Numbers and figures are always stressed e.g. *In 1957,* **six** *countries signed the first agreement.*
   b. Within a long word, stress the syllable before '–tion', before, '-ic', and before '–ity' *e.g.Econ****O****mic Comm****U****nity, add****i****tion*
   c. Stress negatives e.g. *Britain would* **not** *agree to this.*
   d. Abbrevations: stress all of the letters, especially the last e.g. *the* ***EEC***
   e. Do not stress articles ('the, 'a') or auxiliary verbs (unless negative) *e.g. in the phrases 'was ad****O****pted' and 'were r****e****cognised'* stress the verb after the auxiliary verbs *'was/ were'*, not the auxiliary verb itself.
2. Can you memorise the EU story? Try putting sentences against the dates below:
   1957:
   1973:
   1986:
   1992:
   2002:
   2004:
   2013:
   2016:

108. Another extract from a novel

Jane's Secret is set in the early nineteenth century. At the age of sixteen, Jane has attracted the interest of a rich young man, Sir Robert Warren. Her governess accompanies her to a lunchtime meeting with Sir Robert. Don't try to understand every word, but can you understand enough to answer the questions after the text?

Jane was invited to meet Sir Robert for lunch at the Dorchester Hotel. Miss Simpkins would accompany her. The weather was wet and windy, and Jane hoped they may be able to call off the appointment, but the carriage drive was not impossible and they set off as planned.

There was a little discussion of the inclement weather, followed by a brief exchange on what they were going to eat. Jane had been trained to ask what him what he would recommend, and also to say that she would like something light. She was reluctant to take the initiative in conversation, and it was Miss Simpkins who asked Sir Robert about the sugar trade. His account was not altogether to Jane's liking. Sugar was farmed in the West Indies to meet the large demand for it in Britain, but the requirement for labour on the sugar plantations meant that slaves were purchased in Africa for the work. Miss Simpkins enquired as to how much Sir Robert had travelled. He replied that he had so far managed to do his work from an office in London, travelling only to Bristol, where ships arrived with his goods. He was expecting to make a trip to the Caribbean next summer. Given the history of his father's death at sea, he was somewhat nervous about making the journey. The two ladies expressed their condolences at the loss of his father and there was a period where the conversation stopped. Their lunch was served, which prevented the silence from being awkward. It was clear that Sir Robert was a man of few words, but he did venture to ask Jane a question as they finished their soup.

"I should like to know a little more about you, Miss Jane. How do you like to spend your time?"

It sounded like a question he had been primed to ask. Sir Robert was living with his mother, and they suspected that she had advised her son on how he should conduct the luncheon appointment.

"I enjoy the fresh air. I like to walk every day if I can. It might not be possible today with this weather."

Miss Simpkins helped Jane with her answer:

"Jane is very fond of art and music. She also enjoys reading novels."

"I see." The brevity of response suggested that these were not subjects of which Sir Robert had much appreciation.

A main dish was served and eating took the place of conversation for a few minutes, with the exception of comments on the food.

"Is the food to your liking?"

"Yes, thank you, very nice."

When they had all finished eating, Miss Simpkins asked if he had brothers or sisters.

"One of each – quite a bit younger than me. My little brother is thirteen and my sister is eleven."

Feeling that perhaps further explanation was needed, he continued:

"When I was young, my father was away for a long period. He returned home when I was about ten. After that he managed his business from London and just went away for a month at a time. He crossed the Atlantic many times, sadly one time too many."

Again there was an awkward silence, broken by the arrival of a dessert. Sir Robert managed to think of another question for Jane:

"Would you like to travel, Miss Jane?"

"Not so far as to cross the Atlantic. Perhaps to Italy, or Bohemia."

"I see."

(From *Jane's Secret* by Ian Sydenham, published in 2020 on amazon)

1. Describe Jane's enthusiasm for her meeting with Sir Robert.
2. What can you say about Sir Robert's work?
3. What do we learn about Sir Robert's character?
4. What are three things that interest Jane?
5. Fill in the blanks to describe Sir Robert's family: *His _____ passed away in an accident at sea. Sir Robert lives with his _____, his brother and his sister. His brother is _____ years old, and his _____ is eleven.*

Some of the difficult words in the text are on the left: can you match the meanings on the right to fit the words on the left?

reluctant	wishes of consolation
inclement	likes, keen on
condolences	not willing
fond of	start a journey
primed	not pleasant
call off	prepared
set off	postpone or cancel

Imagine you are at a lunch party and ask or answer these questions:

What would you like to eat? What would you recommend?

Can you tell me about your work? How do you like to spend your time?

Do you have any brothers or sisters?

109. Marriage in the twenty-first century

As you read the extract from the novel "Jane's Secret", what were your impressions about marriage in the nineteenth century? Jane was forced to marry Sir Robert, but in Britain in the twenty-first century most people think this is wrong. Read the text below and discuss the topic of marriage in your class or with another person.

Some vocabulary: match the words on the left with the definition on the right:

a wedding	extravagant, elaborate (and costly!)
to get engaged	to live with someone without marrying
to cohabit	the ceremony where you get married
commitment	to formally promise to get married
lavish	the promise of full, unconditional support

Of the population aged 16 and over in England and Wales, just over half were living in a formal marriage relationship or civil partnership in 2020. 13.6% were living together (cohabiting) with a partner without being married. Although this may suggest that most British people prefer marriage to cohabitation, the figures vary according to age, and those under 30 are much less likely to be married.

One reason for this is the cost of many British weddings. Some couples move in together but say "We can't afford to get married yet." This underlines a change from 50-60 years ago, when couples would typically get engaged and arrange a wedding three or four months later. The weddings were still great occasions, though possibly not as lavish as many modern weddings, and the cost of the wedding was traditionally met by the bride's parents. Today couples often meet the wedding costs themselves and want everything to be perfect, meaning that weddings take at least a year to plan and cost thousands of pounds, some will even fly with friends and family to an exotic location to get married on a Caribbean beach or in Las Vegas! It is therefore not surprising that some couples put off the wedding until they are older or drop the idea altogether.

There are, however, a number of important advantages in being married. For the two people involved, marriage is a contract that promises commitment. Many unmarried couples are fully committed to each other, but sometimes at least one of them wants to hear the other promise to stay committed "in sickness and in health" – through the good times and the more difficult times. For the family and friends of the couple (and the public in general), seeing and hearing a statement of their togetherness makes the situation clear: these two people belong together, everyone else should respect them and support them. The legal side of the marriage contract is important too. How many cohabiting couples have come unstuck when things go wrong because they have no legal status as a couple? Many of these benefits can be achieved through civil partnerships too, but in Britain these have largely been employed for couples of the same gender.

Perhaps the act of marriage (which is fundamentally quite simple) needs to be separated from the lavish wedding party, but asking for such a cultural change is probably not realistic.

As you discuss, you might use these expressions, but try to respect the opinion of other people even if you don't agree!

To express surprise:

Really?

That's strange.

That's different!

To express agreement:

Absolutely!

Totally!

That's right.

To express disagreement (politely!)

I can't agree with that.

No, I don't think that's right.

Use one of the expressions above to react to these statements:

"Women should be paid the same as men if they do the same job".

"In my country women must wear a head covering outside the house".

"We should execute all criminals- it would save a lot of money!".

"Couples of the same gender should be allowed to get married".

"It's better to have a republic than a monarchy".

Work with a partner and say some controversial things! You can say things you don't really believe and say afterwards "Don't worry" That's not my opinion!"

110. More phrasal verbs

(Look at the unit on Phrasal Verbs)

In the last unit we read about marriage. Sadly, some couples separate – more commonly we use the phrasal verb "break up". Here are some more phrasal verbs (verbs with two or more parts): Can you see where they fit?

break down	catch up	check in	check out	fill in
call back	find out	get back	give up	go over	let in
let out	look after	look for	put on	take off (2)	run out of
sort out	throw away	turn on	turn off	wake up	warm up

1. To search for something: *I can't find my passport – I need to ___ ___ it.*
2. To set a machine in motion: *You ___ ___ the printer by pushing the blue button.*
3. To return a phone call: *I'm busy now – can I ___ you ___?*
4. To release from captivity: *I was detained for two weeks before they ___ me ___.*
5. When a machine stops working: *Let's hope the car doesn't ___ ___!*
6. To research information: *I don't know, but I will ___ ___.*
7. To put in the rubbish bin: *That's no good any more, you can ___ it ___.*
8. To get dressed in something: *It's cold - ___ ___ your thick coat!*
9. To return: *What time will you ___ ___ ?*
10. To get up to date after missing something e.g. a lesson: *If you weren't here last week, you will need to ___ ___.*
11. To take care of: *Don't worry, I will ___ ___ her while you are away.*
12. To register (e.g. in a hotel/ airport): *what time do we have to ___ ___ ?*
13. To stop a machine, or a tap: *I forgot to ___ ___ the tap – now there's water everywhere!*
14. To allow to enter: *I've forgotten my key – can you ___ me ___, please?*
15. To complete (e.g. an application form): *Could you ___ ___ your details here, please?*
16. To tell someone you are leaving (e.g. a hotel): *Please return the key when you ___ ___.*
17. To stop sleeping: *___ ___! It's time to get ready for school!*
18. To stop trying: *I can't find the answer, I ___ ___.*
19. To explain, repeat more clearly: You have five minutes, then I will ___ ___ the answers.
20. To prepare your body (e.g. before sport): *Before we start, let's ___ ___.*
21. To put things in order: *I have a lot of documents here, but I need to ___ them ___.*
22. To remove a piece of clothing: *___ ___ your shoes, please, we have a new carpet!*
23. To not have any more: *We've ___ ___ ___ sugar – can you get some more, please?*
24. (for a plane) To leave the ground: *Our plane ___ ___ at 18.30.*

111. Those were the days! – a song

(You will need to find the text for this song on the internet. You can probably listen to it too!)

Language:

What are the verb tenses used in the song?

We used to raise a glass...

We use 'used to' for something that was often or sometimes the situation in the past e.g.

I used to live in London.

We used to play football in that park

What do you think "We'd" is short for?

Answer: "We would"

This is similar to "We used to" – it means it was our habit at that time.

What are the verb tenses in the last verse? The change is important to understand the song!

What is it about?

Talk with other people on your table. What do you think is the age of the person writing the song? Who is he speaking to?

Until the last verse, what is the atmosphere? Choose one of these adjectives:

happy   nostalgic   sad   romantic   protesting

In the last verse, what is the atmosphere?

Why not try singing the song in your class?

112. A difficult decision (other conditional sentences)

Read this conversation between two friends...

Person A: Hello. How are you doing?

Person B: Fine, thank you, and you?

Person A: I'm OK. But I've got a difficult decision to make.

Person B: Oh? What's that then?

Person A: I went for a job interview this morning, and they said if I wanted the job, I would have to tell them by the end of today.

Person B: I see. Did you like the job?

Person A: I'm not sure. I have an interview for another job next Monday. If I accepted the job today, I would have to cancel the interview next week.

Person B: Do you think the job next week would be better?

Person A: I'm not sure. If I went to the interview, I would know more about it.

Person B: If I were* you, I would tell the people you saw today to wait for an answer. If they can't wait, they are not flexible and I wouldn't want to work for them.

Person A : Maybe, but if I said 'No' to them and then I didn't get offered the job next week, I would end up with nothing.

Person B: Mmm, I can see it's difficult. If you would like to talk some more, give me a ring later. I have to go now.

Person A: Of course. Sorry, I shouldn't have bothered you with my problems.

Person B: Not at all! I wouldn't have been pleased if you hadn't told me. I'm sorry not to have been more helpful.

Person A: Don't worry, I'll figure it out. I'll tell the people I saw this morning that I would like more time and see what they say.

Person B: That sounds like a good idea. See you soon!

Person A: Bye!

*The conversation is full of conditional "if" clauses. Most of them are what we sometimes call **"Second conditional"** – "if" clause has the past simple, main clause has "would + verb".*

If I accepted the job today, I would have to cancel the interview next week.

If I went to the interview, I would know more about it.

It is used for something that is not sure, not decided yet, hypothetical. Here are a couple of other examples:

I would go to the USA if I had the money. (*The main clause comes first here*).

If you wanted a second opinion, you could ask a different dentist. (*In this example, "could" is used – we never say ~~would can~~: "would be able to" is also possible*).

*"If I were you" is a traditional phrase, but many people today say "If I was you"

Try to complete these sentences – what do you need to do with the verb in brackets?

If I (have) the time, I (study) more. At the moment I am very busy. I (be able to) get a better job if I (get) more qualifications. Then I (buy) some new clothes if I (earn) more money.

*The "**Third conditional**" is used when it is too late, when we regret that something is not the case.*

I wouldn't have been pleased if you hadn't told me. (*You did tell me so it's OK!*)

The "if" clause has the past perfect ("had" + past participle), the main clause has "would have" + past participle.

"could have" and "should have" are also used in Third conditionals:

I shouldn't have bothered you with my problems. (*Too late! I've told you now!*)

You could have asked me if you had needed a babysitter. (*The situation has passed*).

("would/could/should have + past participle is an example of a three-word tense - see the verb notes at the back of the book. It is sometimes referred to as a "conditional perfect").

113. Census 2021- Religion in Britain (who/which)

Read this text about the 2021 census:

The census is a survey which takes place every ten years. It is compulsory to take part in the census, but there are some questions which are voluntary. For example, you have to give the details and ages of all the people who live in the property (house, flat, hotel etc.) on a specific date. This means that the census can provide accurate information on the population.

One of the voluntary questions is about religion. If they belong to a religious faith group, the census asks which group they belong to. Although this question is not compulsory, 94% of the people who replied to the census answered the question about religion.

There were just over 46% who said they were Christian. The second biggest group were the people who said they had no religion – over 37%. This was a big increase on the census ten years earlier. 6.5% identified as Muslim, and there were 1.7% who said they were Hindu. Sikhs made up 0.9% of the population, and those who describe themselves as Jewish or Buddhist made up 0.5% each.

These figures are averages for England and Wales.

Check your understanding by completing these sentences:

Taking part in the census in 2021 was _____, but the questions about religion were _____.

Just over 46% of people describe themselves as _____.

There are _____ people who say they have no religion compared to 2011.

About _____% of people describe themselves as Jewish.

The statistics describe people in England and _____.

Who, which etc.

Read the text again and find examples of the words 'who' and 'which'.

We use these words to make our sentences more interesting. We could say:

You have to give details of all the people.

The people live in the property.

*But it is better to join the sentences: the word **'who' refers to the people** and is the subject of the verb 'live' in the second half of the sentence:*

You have to give details of all the people **who** live in the property.

We could make two sentences:

The census is a survey.

It takes place every ten years.

But we can use "which" to join the sentences together:

The census is a survey **which** takes place every ten years.

"who" refers back to a person (or people), "which" refers back to a thing (or things)

In the text below, insert the word 'who' or 'which':

There is a large diversity of religious belief in Britain, _____ is particularly the case in London. The people ___ say they have no religion now make up more than a third of the population. The term 'atheist is used to describe someone ___ does not believe in God. Religious Education is a subject _____ is taught in all schools, and many schools are supported by the Church of England or other faith groups, _____ you will normally see from the name of the school.

114. Two more texts for discussion

On the next two pages are texts about space exploration and GM crops: These are for you to discuss in your class or just to practise your English with friends. There are no questions or exercises on the texts, but you can use them to start a conversation about the subject (or topic). You could find other texts too (for example, from a newspaper, magazine or web page) and use the ideas here to practise your English with a range of topics.

You could use these questions:
What is the text about?
What does the author want to tell us?
Is there an argument for or against something?
Which parts of the text do you agree with?
Which parts don't you agree with?
What is your opinion on the subject?

If the subject is controversial, you could try to set up a debate: one person gives one side of the argument, another gives the other side, others can ask questions …(look back at the unit on "Marriage in the twenty-first century" for language on agreeing and disagreeing).

Where the text lists a number of options, you could discuss which you think is best, and what are the advantages and disadvantages of the things mentioned.

You could also look at the language of the text. Which verb tenses are used and why? Are there examples of phrasal verbs, or conditional clauses, or 'who/which' clauses?

To the moon and beyond

In the late 1960s American astronauts landed on the moon. There has been a recent revival in interest in space exploration, partly because of private entrepreneurs suggesting a voyage into space as a tourist adventure. The American Space Agency, NASA, has also started a new moon programme. Journeys to the moon became unpopular after some tragic accidents and some near misses (as shown in the film *Apollo 13,* based on the real events of that particular mission to the moon). Furthermore, there was criticism of the expense of the space programme, and concerns that both the USA and the Soviet Union were using their space programme for military purposes.
There have been benefits to our lives achieved through space exploration, notably the satellite technology which we rely on for our communications and entertainment, but some opponents question how many significant advantages have been gained through the missions to the moon and into space. There is of course a curiosity that drives space exploration, a fascination with planets and solar systems, and the inevitable question as to whether there are aliens. Science fiction has been popular in literature and even more popular at the cinema box office. Space exploration has developed steadily, even if manned space missions have not grabbed the public attention in the way that the Apollo programme did when men first landed on the moon. A number of countries have now sent satellites into space, and it is possible that the next big discoveries in space will be made by a new player in global space exploration.

Genetically Modified crops

Cereals, fruit and vegetables that can resist insects, crops that can grow even in drought conditions, products that contain extra vitamins or even vaccines against certain diseases, the ability to grow produce to better satisfy consumer demand... the list of possibilities offered by genetic modification is constantly growing. Genetically modified (GM) foods are foods whose genetic material (DNA) has been modified in a way that does not occur naturally, e.g. through the introduction of a gene from a different organism.

Corn, soya, potatoes, rice and cotton are already being produced in some countries with GM technology. Improving the yield of crops could be a major help in preventing famine, and GM farming could reduce the cost of food. Nevertheless, GM food is not without its opponents. Some object to playing with nature, others are concerned by the way some companies monopolise the field, even preventing their crops from being re-used (so that customers need to purchase again each year). Many countries have been cautious in allowing GM farming, but there can be little doubt that the technology will play a major part in the future of feeding the world's population.

115. More on the order of words

(Most English people don't know this, but they know that it sounds wrong to say "green little men" or "bad, big wolf"!)

Where you a have a group of words that go together (normally adjectives that go with a noun), the stressed vowel follows the order **i– a – o**

So the fairy tale villain is the "**bi**g b**a**d w**o**lf", we sometimes say "let's have a s**i**ng-s**o**ng", the clock goes "t**i**ck-t**o**ck" and there is a sweet called "T**i**c-T**a**cs".

There is also an order we use for more than one adjective:

opinion – size – age – shape – colour – origin – material – purpose

So sometimes aliens are referred to a "little green men" because size comes before colour.

Look at these examples and see how they follow the rule:

A beautiful old building

A yellow cycling jacket

An old French painting

A round baking tin

It is unusual to have more than two adjectives, but it's possible!

We have a lovely little old rectangular brown Dutch wooden dining table!

But the i-a-o rule wins in the phrase "big bad wolf"!

Put the two words at the end into these sentences in the correct order:

1. That's a dress (little, nice)
2. It's a village (beautiful, old)
3. We have a car (German, new)
4. It's a football match (dong, ding)
5. You need a helmet. (new, cycling)

Grammar pages

This is not a complete grammar of English! It just deals with two important areas of learning:

- *Different types of word (noun, verb, adjectiveetc.)*
- *Verb tenses*

Use them as reference, but the first section also has an exercise so that you can test yourself on how much you know already about different types of word.

116. Types of word

You will meet these terms:

- Noun (and Proper Noun)
- Verb
- Article
- Pronoun
- Adjective
- Preposition
- Conjunction
- Adverb

What do you know already? In this text, some of the words have a number. Can you identify which of the categories above describes the numbered words? The first one has been answered for you as an example. Then look through the explanations below to check your answers.

Caroline (1) is a teacher in Birmingham. She works (2) in a school (3) near the city centre. It is a large(4) secondary school with about 1200 pupils. The(5) pupils are sometimes difficult, but (6) generally she likes her job. She lives in Solihull (7) with her husband and two children. Her husband is called Pete. He (8) is self-employed – he helps people with their computer problems. He always (9) has plenty of work. The two children are both teenagers, and the eldest, Donna, does not live at (10) home with her parents because (11) she is at university (12) in Leeds.

1. Proper Noun	2.	3.
4.	5.	6.
7.	8.	9.
10.	11.	12.

211

Nouns (and Proper Nouns)

A noun can be a person, a thing, a job, something to eat, a place (such as 'school' in the text above, so for number 3 the answer was *Noun*), an idea... These words are all nouns: pizza, people, town, restaurant, waiter, bread, trousers, communication, television, news, and many more!

Most nouns can be singular or plural*. When they are singular they are normally used with the articles "a" or "the" (see the section on *Articles* below), and when they are plural, they may have "the" or be used without an article. Most nouns add -s to make the plural, but there are a few exceptions.

A proper noun is the name of a person, an organisation, the title of something (film, book, play, TV programme...) or a place . The word always starts with a capital letter, for example, London, New York, Christopher, MacDonalds, China, Americans, Top Gun, Pride and Prejudice,... Number 1, the example in the text above, is a proper noun, and number 7 – Solihull – is also a proper noun.

Go back to the text above and identify the other nouns and proper nouns with your teacher.

*There are some nouns which cannot have a plural. They are referred to as 'Uncountable' nouns. "Bread" is an example of an Uncountable noun. We will look at this in another lesson.

Verbs

Verbs are "doing words" – they describe the action that you, another person, or a noun take. The verb is highlighted in these sentences:

Mo **likes** folk music and **plays** the guitar. She **has** a wonderful voice, and **performs** regularly in pubs and folk clubs in the area where she **lives**.

The verb 'to be' (*am/is/are* in the present tense) may not describe an action, but it is still a verb!

Number 2 in the exercise above – 'works' – is a verb. Can you identify the other verbs in the text? Every sentence must have a verb.

Words like 'can', 'will', 'must', 'may', 'should' are a special type of verb called 'modal verbs': they are used with another verb.

Will you watch TV this evening? I should study for my exams, but I will watch my favourite programme for half an hour.

Articles

The little words 'a' ('an' before a vowel) and 'the' are called articles. Some languages have no articles, others use them more than English (plural nouns and uncount nouns are often used with no article), so it is understandable that learners of English to find them difficult to use correctly. They are not very important words, but try to master them!

Number 5 in the above exercise is an article ('the'): can you identify the other articles in the text?

Pronouns

A pronoun takes the place of a noun or proper noun so that we don't repeat the same words:

Shepherd's Pie is a typical English dish. **It** is made of meat in sauce covered with mashed potato and **it** is grilled to brown the top.

In this example the pronoun 'it' replaces 'Shepherd's Pie' when it is repeated. In the text above, number 8 – the word 'he' – is a pronoun. Can you find other pronouns in the text about Caroline?

Subject pronouns	*Object pronouns*
I	*me*
you	*you*
he/she/it	*him/her/it*
we	*us*
they	*them*

Adjectives

Adjectives are describing words, and they are placed before the noun they describe (or used with the verb 'to be'). There are adjectives of size, quality, and many other types. These words are all adjectives:

big, small, beautiful, young, old, fantastic, amazing, interesting, important…

Here is the text about Caroline again:

Caroline (1) is a teacher in Birmingham. She works (2) in a school (3) near the city centre. It is a large(4) secondary school with about 1200 pupils. The(5) pupils are sometimes difficult, but (6) generally she likes her job. She lives in Solihull (7) with her husband and two children. Her husband is called Pete. He (8) is self-employed – he helps people with their computer problems. He always (9) has plenty of work. The two children are both teenagers, and the eldest, Donna, does not live at (10) home with her parents because (11) she is at university (12) in Leeds.

Number 4 – the word 'large' – is an adjective. Can you find any other adjectives in the text? The phrase 'computer problems' is interesting – 'computer' is a noun, but it is used here like an adjective. We often find this in English e.g. 'a football team', 'a film star', 'the town centre'…

Prepositions

Words used with a noun, often to describe position (in, on, at, over, under, next to*, behind, in front of*, near, opposite…).

Other common prepositions include:

to, about, for, by, with, of, from, out of*, before, after, until, between, in spite of* …

(*You can see that some prepositions have more than one word.)

In the text, number 10 – 'at' – is a preposition. Can you find others? There are at least 8 more!)

Conjunctions

Conjunctions join sentences or phrases together. The simplest example is 'and': *I like playing tennis and I also like watching it on TV.*

'but' is used in a similar way if one of the two phrases is negative: *I eat meat but I don't like lamb.*

We just saw another important conjunction – 'if'.

In the text above, number 11 – the word 'because' – is a conjunction. There are many more possible conjunctions, for example, most question words can be used as conjunctions:

When you come to my house, I will show you my paintings.

This is the room where I keep my paintings.

I don't know how long I will stay here.

Adverbs

Adverbs give extra information about the verb e.g. I got dressed **quickly**.

We can make most adjectives into adverbs by adding -ly:

Adjective: slow – *This is a slow train.*

Adverb: slowly – *Can you speak slowly, please*?

Adverbs of frequency are very useful: *always/sometimes/often/normally/ rarely/ never*

In the text above, number 9 – the word 'always'- is an adverb. What other adverbs are there in the text?

117. Summary of verbs in English

(There is a lot to read here. Find a text in English and study the verbs, trying to find which tense is used by looking for it in the notes below. To get you started, you could use the text in Unit 107 about the European Union)

The present simple tense:

Form: the verb (+ s if you refer to another person/thing or 'he/she/it')

Irregular: am/is/are (the verb 'to be')

~~haves~~ → has

Use: describing a present situation

I *play* tennis every Tuesday in Bilton. It *is* a village near Rugby. One of the other players *comes* from Africa.

Negatives and questions: use **do/does (not)+ verb** (except the verb 'to be')

The past simple tense:

Form: add -ed to verb

Irregular: many verbs have an irregular form (see section 24)

Use: past events and description

I l*ived* in Essex as a boy. I *went* to school in Brentwood. I *met* my wife at university. We *got* married in 1981...

Negatives and questions: use did (not) + verb (except 'to be': was not, were not

Modal verbs:

The most common are will, can, must, may, shall

Use: always with another verb to add something (e.g. ability – can, future – will/shall, obligation – must...)

Negatives and questions: no ~~do/does~~ – e.g. Can I help you? You must not sit there! May I sit here? I will not be at the lesson tomorrow

Past modals:

1. The forms 'would, could, should, might' exist but need to be used carefully.
2. It is normally safer to use alternatives to make the past tense of modals:
   e.g. *must* in the present → *had to* in the past
   can in the present → *was able to* in the past

Present Perfect:

Form: 'have/has + past participle'

Regular past participle is **verb + -ed**, but many verbs are irregular (see section 40 for a few examples)

Use: experiences which started in the past and continue or are likely to be repeated again e.g. *How many times have you been to London? I have never been there. How long have you lived here? I have studied English for six years.*

Negatives and questions: no ~~do/does~~ (see examples above)

Take note: "have got" is used as an alternative to "have" in the present simple: *Have you got a pen? I haven't got any cash, have you?*

Past perfect:

Form: 'had + past participle'

Use: in a series of verbs in the past, the past perfect is used for something that happened before other verbs.

*I left my house and went to the car. Then I realised that I **had forgotten** my keys, so I returned to the house and found them.*

Present continuous (or present progressive):

Form: 'am/is/are + verb-ing'

Use: to describe something that is happening now, at this moment, that will probably not last long. Occasionally it is used for a near future. The form 'am/is/are going to + verb' is useful as an alternative to 'will' particularly used for something that is quite definite in the near future.

- *Where are you going?*
- *I am going into town. Would you like to come with me?*
- *No thanks. I'm going to change my clothes, then I'm playing football with my friends in half an hour.*

Past continuous (or past progressive):

Form: 'was/were + verb -ing'

Use: setting a scene in the past (where most verbs are in the past simple) e.g.

*I **was sitting** at my desk yesterday afternoon when my phone rang. It was a friend. We chatted for twenty minutes and he suggested we meet in town, but it **was raining** and I told him I preferred to stay at home.*

Passive Present:

Form: am/is/are + past participle

Use: where the subject receives the verb; often when it is not so important who does the action

*Rugby **is played** in about twenty countries.*

I am interested in the position of administrative assistant.

(The past participle is like an adjective, for example *Are you married? I am surprised*)

Past passive:

Form: was/were + past participle

Use: as with the present passive, but describing a past situation

*Fifteen people **were injured** in the accident.*

*He **was seen** in the garden this morning.*

Combinations:

You can have combinations of the above to make **three-word tenses** or even **four-word tenses**!

*How long **have** you **been learning** English?* (three-word tense combining the present perfect and progressive)

*He **should have listened** to his mother's advice!* (three-word tense combining the modal 'should' with the present perfect)

*I **would have been playing** tennis now but I've injured my arm.* (four-word tense combining a modal, present perfect and progressive)

Present Simple	Past Simple
Modals (present)	Modals (past)
Present Perfect	Past Perfect
Present Continuous	Past Continuous
Passive (present)	Passive (past)
3-word	4-word

Finally, here is a table of common irregular verbs. You will have to learn these. There are some patterns, but it isn't easy to know which verbs follow which pattern! Notice that if the verb combines another verb with a prefix (come/become, stand/understand, get/forget...), the irregular forms follow the same pattern as the basic verb.

Present verb	Past simple	Past participle
am/is /are (to be)	was/were	been
do/does	did	done
have	had	had
go	went	gone
see	saw	seen
come	came	come
speak	spoke	spoken
eat	ate	eaten
drink	drank	drunk
sleep	slept	slept
(under)stand	(under)stood)	(under)stood
(for)get	(for)got	(for)got/forgotten
lose	lost	lost
give	gave	given
know	knew	known
read	read ['red']	read ['red']
take	took	taken
tell	told	told
say	said ['sed']	said ['sed']
make	made	made
send	sent	sent
leave	left	left
hear	heard	heard
sing	sang	sung
ring	rang	rung
buy	bought	bought
bring	brought	brought
fight	fought	fought
teach	taught	taught
meet	met	met
grow	grew	grown

Printed in Great Britain
by Amazon